MOVIE ★ ICONS

BOGART

EDITOR
PAUL DUNCAN

TEXT
JAMES URSINI

PHOTOS
THE KOBAL COLLECTION

TASCHEN

HONG KONG KÖLN LONDON LOS ANGELES MADRID PARIS TOKYO

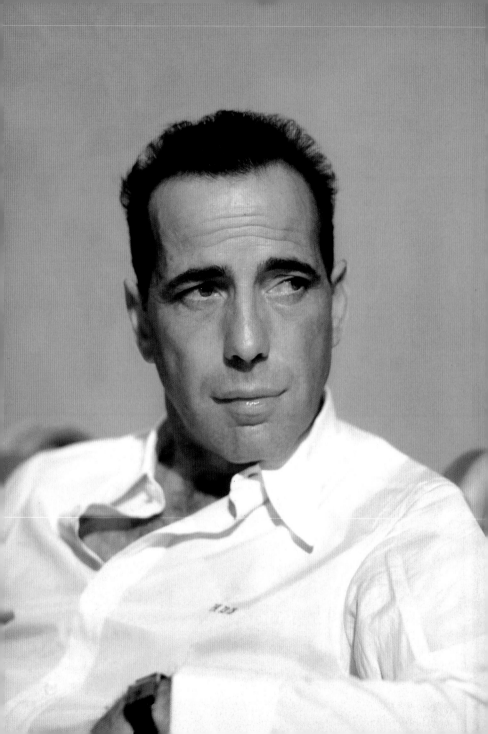

CONTENTS

1

HUMPHREY BOGART: TOUGH GUY

BY JAMES URSINI

HUMPHREY BOGART: DER KNALLHARTE

HUMPHREY BOGART : LE DUR À CUIRE

HUMPHREY BOGART: TOUGH GUY

by James Ursini

For centuries religious icons symbolized ideal virtues, such as purity, holiness, and devotion. In the modern age, a secular world has replaced the idols of old with celebrities and called them "icons." Humphrey Bogart is such an icon. He incarnates the modern virtues of toughness and integrity that speak culturally and emotionally to the fantasy of his audiences. But to become a true icon and maintain a fan base of worshipers decades after your demise, one must also be human—that is, reflect some of the vulnerabilities and weaknesses the fans see in themselves.

Icons are not born fully formed. It often takes decades to develop an image people will fasten on to. Bogart started his career in the theater, often playing upper-class, genteel characters, reflecting his own privileged family background as well as his soft youthful good looks. He met with mild success in these early theatrical forays, but Bogart felt trapped by typecasting. When he finally made his way west to Hollywood in 1930, he did not fare any better. The parts he was given at Fox and later at Columbia were "inconsequential" and "fluff," according to the actor himself. And so he returned to New York and the stage.

The role in which Bogart single-handedly molded the 'tough guy' image that audiences came to idolize was that of Duke Mantee in Robert E. Sherwood's play *The Petrified Forest*. On stage in 1935 and later in the film version in 1936, Bogart cut himself off irrevocably from his upper-class background, drawing instead on his frustration as an actor and his combativeness (which was, even then, notorious) to personify a complex gangster who alternated between violence and depression and whose face and posture registered angst.

Although Bogart found critical success in the role of Duke Mantee, Warner Bros., who now owned his contract, continued to relegate him to mostly one-dimensional roles as heavies

PORTRAIT FOR 'HIGH SIERRA' (1941)
Bogart in his breakout role as aging gangster Roy "Mad Dog" Earle. / Bogart in seiner Rolle als alternder Gangster Roy „Mad Dog" Earle, mit der ihm der Durchbruch gelang. / Bogart dans le rôle qui l'a rendu célèbre, celui du gangster vieillissant Roy Earle.

"There he is, right there on the screen, saying what everyone is trying to say today, saying it loud and clear: 'I hate hypocrisy. I don't believe in words and labels or much of anything else. I'm not a hero. I'm a human being.'"
Mary Astor

(*Angels with Dirty Faces* (1938), *The Roaring Twenties* (1939), *Brother Orchid* (1940), etc.), often second-billed to fellow actors James Cagney and Edward. G. Robinson. Bogart fought the studio tooth and nail as did fellow "indentured servants" (in Bogart's words) like Bette Davis.

At the same time Bogart's personal life was in chaos. Always attracted to strong, aggressive women much like his mother, he found his third wife, actress Mayo Methot, more than he could handle. Although they both drank heavily, fought loudly, and loved passionately, they also had a creative partnership. Bogart listened to her advice, as she encouraged him to continue to fight for more challenging roles. Their perseverance paid off when he got to play aging gangster Roy Earle in *High Sierra* (1941) after both Paul Muni and George Raft turned down the role. The film was a critical and financial success and led to Bogart's next two landmark roles: one with writer-director John Huston, that of Dashiell Hammett's hardboiled detective Sam Spade in *The Maltese Falcon* (1941); and his most iconic role, that of Rick Blaine, the alienated expatriate in *Casablanca* (1942). With these key roles Bogart refined his angst-filled tough guy role as well as setting the standard for the film noir protagonist of the 1940s.

Bogart continued to tweak his noirish persona for the rest of his career, often in conjunction with his last and most famous wife, actress/model Lauren Bacall, another strong woman. With Bacall he not only made three noir classics (*To Have and Have Not* (1944), *The Big Sleep* (1946), and *Dark Passage* (1947)) but also helped organize a group of film personalities who traveled to Washington D.C. to protest the Red 'witch hunts' fostered by Senator Joseph McCarthy and the House Un-American Activities Committee. Acts like this, even though controversial within the frightened film industry, contributed to Bogart's iconic status, the iconoclast who defended the underdog.

In 1952 his peers finally honored his iconic status as well as his acting skills with an Academy Award for his performance in John Huston's *The African Queen* (1951). He also received rave critical reviews for his portrayal of Queeg, the psychotic commander in *The Caine Mutiny* (1954). Although Bogart died of cancer in 1957, these performances cemented his legend. His legend did not die with him. How could it? He was an icon.

HUMPHREY BOGART: DER KNALLHARTE

von James Ursini

Jahrhundertelang standen religiöse Ikonen für Ideale wie Tugendhaftigkeit, Reinheit und Hingabe. Heutzutage haben wir die alten Vorbilder durch weltliche Prominenz ersetzt, für die wir ebenfalls den Begriff „Ikone" verwenden. Humphrey Bogart ist eine solche Ikone. Er verkörpert moderne Tugenden wie Härte und Integrität, die kulturell wie emotional die Phantasie seines Publikums ansprechen. Um jedoch zu einer wahren Ikone zu werden und noch Jahrzehnte nach dem Tod eine beachtliche Fangemeinde bei der Stange zu halten, muss man auch Mensch sein – mit anderen Worten: Man muss einen Teil der Schwächen und der Verwundbarkeit zeigen, die die Fans in sich selbst finden.

Ikonen werden nicht als solche geboren. Oft dauert es Jahrzehnte, bis sie ein Image entwickelt haben, an dem sich die Menschen festhalten können. Bogart begann seine Karriere auf der Bühne, wo er häufig vornehme Charaktere spielte, die wie er selbst aus der privilegierten Oberschicht stammten. Seine sanften, jugendlichen Zügen passten zu diesen Rollen, und seine Gehversuche auf der Bühne waren auch nicht ganz erfolglos, doch Bogart fühlte sich künstlerisch eingeengt, weil man ihn schon früh in eine Schublade gesteckt hatte. Als er 1930 schließlich den Sprung nach Hollywood wagte, erging es ihm dort nicht viel besser. Die Rollen, die man ihm bei Fox und später bei Columbia anbot, waren „belanglos" und „nichtssagend", wie er selbst meinte. Und so kehrte er nach New York zurück und auf die Bretter, die die Welt bedeuten.

Die Rolle, mit der sich Bogart auf einen Schlag das Image des knallharten, abgebrühten Typen zulegte, von dem das Publikum später so begeistert war, war die des Duke Mantee in Robert E. Sherwoods Drama *Der versteinerte Wald*. Bogart löste sich 1935 auf der Bühne und im Jahr darauf in der Verfilmung unwiderruflich von seiner Herkunft und verarbeitete stattdessen seine Frustration als Schauspieler und seine bereits damals berüchtigte Streitlust, um eine komplexe Gangsterfigur zu schaffen, die zwischen Brutalität und Depressivität schwankte und deren Gesicht und Haltung Existenzangst ausdrückte.

PORTRAIT (1930)
Bogart demonstrates his more vulnerable, almost effete side in this early portrait. / Bogart zeigt in diesem frühen Porträt seine verletzlichere, fast kraftlose Seite. / Portrait de jeunesse dévoilant un Bogart plus vulnérable, presque indolent.

„Da steht er – genau dort auf der Leinwand – und spricht klar und deutlich aus, was heutzutage alle auszudrücken versuchen: ‚Ich hasse Heuchelei. Ich glaube nicht an Worte und Etiketten oder solche Dinge. Ich bin kein Held. Ich bin ein Mensch.'"
Mary Astor

Obwohl Bogart in der Rolle des Duke Mantee von den Kritikern gefeiert wurde, gab ihm Warner Bros., wo er damals unter Vertrag stand, weiterhin hauptsächlich eindimensionale Schurkenrollen in Filmen wie *Chikago - Engel mit schmutzigen Gesichtern* (1938), *Die wilden Zwanziger* (1939) oder *Orchid, der Gangsterbruder* (1940), bei denen er hinter Kollegen wie James Cagney und Edward G. Robinson die zweite Geige spielte. Bogart und andere (in seinen Worten) „Zwangsarbeiter" wie Bette Davis wehrten sich mit Händen und Füßen gegen diese Besetzungspolitik.

Zur gleichen Zeit ging es in Bogarts Privatleben drunter und drüber. Er fühlte sich stets zu Frauen hingezogen, die ähnlich stark und aggressiv waren wie seine Mutter, aber mit seiner dritten Ehefrau, der Schauspielerin Mayo Methot, hatte er sich offenbar übernommen. Obwohl sich beide gern betranken, lauthals stritten und leidenschaftlich liebten, bildeten sie auch ein kreatives Team. Bogart folgte ihrem Rat, sich um anspruchsvollere Rollen zu bemühen. Die Hartnäckigkeit zahlte sich schließlich aus, als er den alternden Gangster Roy Earle in *Entscheidung in der Sierra* (1941) spielen durfte, nachdem sowohl Paul Muni als auch George Raft die Rolle abgelehnt hatten. Der Film war bei den Kritikern ebenso erfolgreich wie an der Kinokasse und brachte Bogart zwei weitere Rollen ein, die Filmgeschichte schrieben: als Dashiell Hammetts hartgesottener Detektiv Sam Spade in *Die Spur des Falken* (aka *Der Malteser Falke*, 1941) unter der Regie von Autor und Regisseur John Huston sowie seine unvergessliche Rolle als Rick Blaine, dem entfremdeten Exilamerikaner in *Casablanca* (1942). Mit diesen drei Schlüsselrollen gestaltete Bogart seine Rolle des von Existenzängsten erfüllten „harten Kerls" weiter aus und schuf zugleich das Vorbild für die Protagonisten der „schwarzen Serie" in den vierziger Jahren.

Im Verlauf seiner weiteren Karriere gab Bogart der Figur ihren letzten Schliff, oft in Zusammenarbeit mit seiner letzten und berühmtesten Ehefrau, Lauren Bacall, Schauspielerin, Fotomodell und ebenfalls wieder eine starke Frau. Mit Bacall drehte er nicht nur drei Klassiker des *Film noir* (*Haben und Nichthaben* [1944], *Tote schlafen fest* [aka *Der tiefe Schlaf*, 1946] und *Das unbekannte Gesicht* [aka *Die schwarze Natter/Ums eigene Leben*, 1947]), sondern stellte auch eine Delegation von Persönlichkeiten aus dem Filmgeschäft zusammen, die mit dem Ehepaar in die Bundeshauptstadt Washington reiste, um dort gegen die „Hexenjagd" auf Kommunisten zu protestieren, die Senator Joseph McCarthy mit seinem Ausschuss zur Untersuchung unamerikanischer Umtriebe veranstaltete. Obwohl solche Aktionen in der eher ängstlichen Filmindustrie umstritten waren, trugen sie dazu bei, dass sich Bogarts Status als Ikone festigte: Er war nun der Bilderstürmer, der sich für die Schwachen einsetzte.

Im Jahre 1952 fand er schließlich bei seinen Kollegen die verdiente Anerkennung - als Ikone und als Schauspieler - in Form eines „Academy Awards" („Oscars") für seine Leistung in John Hustons *African Queen* (1951). Die Kritiker feierten ihn auch in seiner Rolle als Queeg, den geistig verwirrten Schiffsführer in *Die Caine war ihr Schicksal* (1954). Als Bogart 1957 an Krebs starb, hatten diese Rollen längst eine Legende geschaffen, die ihn lange überdauerte. Wie hätte es auch anders sein können? Er war schließlich eine Ikone.

PORTRAIT FOR 'CASABLANCA' (1942)
A smiling Bogart in his iconic white tux. / Ein lächelnder Bogart in seinem typischen weißen Smoking. / Bogart souriant dans son légendaire smoking blanc.

HUMPHREY BOGART: LE DUR À CUIRE

James Ursini

Pendant des siècles, les icônes religieuses ont symbolisé des vertus idéales telles que la pureté, la sainteté et la dévotion. À l'époque moderne, notre société laïque a remplacé les anciens objets de culte par des célébrités auxquelles elle donne le nom ... d'icônes. Humphrey Bogart est l'une d'elles. Il incarne des vertus modernes – ténacité et intégrité – qui trouvent un écho culturel et émotionnel dans l'imaginaire du public. Mais pour devenir un véritable mythe et conserver une foule d'adorateurs des décennies après sa mort, il faut également faire preuve d'humanité, c'est-à-dire refléter une part des faiblesses et de la vulnérabilité que les admirateurs ressentent au fond d'eux-mêmes.

Les icônes ne naissent pas icônes. Il faut souvent des décennies pour forger l'image à laquelle le public s'attachera. Bogart a débuté sa carrière au théâtre, souvent cantonné dans des personnages distingués reflétant son milieu favorisé et son physique de jeune premier. Malgré le vague succès que lui valent ses premiers pas sur les planches, Bogart se sent enfermé dans un rôle. Mais lorsqu'il arrive enfin à Hollywood en 1930, il déchante rapidement. Les rôles que lui confient la Fox puis Columbia sont «légers» et «inconséquents», selon ses propres termes. Il reprend donc le chemin des théâtres new-yorkais.

Le rôle dans lequel Bogart parvient à forger l'image de «dur à cuire» que le public va idolâtrer est celui de Duke Mantee dans la pièce de Robert E. Sherwood, *La Forêt pétrifiée*. D'abord sur scène en 1935, puis dans l'adaptation cinématographique en 1936, Bogart rompt définitivement avec ses origines huppées. Il puise dans sa frustration d'acteur ainsi que dans sa combativité (déjà notoire à l'époque) pour incarner un personnage complexe de gangster oscillant entre la violence et la dépression, dont le visage et la posture trahissent une véritable angoisse existentielle.

Malgré le succès critique que lui vaut le personnage de Duke Mantee, la Warner Bros., dont il dépend désormais, continue à le reléguer dans des rôles simplistes de truand. Dans des films comme *Les Anges aux figures sales* (1938), *Les Fantastiques Années 20* (1939) et *Brother*

PORTRAIT
Bogart projects the dark, angst-ridden persona which made him a noir star. / Bogart in der Rolle der düstern, von Existenzangst geplagten Figur, die ihn zu einem Star des *Film noir* machte. / Le personnage ténébreux et torturé qui a fait de lui une star du film noir.

« Là, sous nos yeux, il dit haut et fort ce que tout le monde essaie de dire aujourd'hui : "Je déteste l'hypocrisie. Je ne crois ni aux paroles, ni aux étiquettes, ni à grand-chose d'autre. Je ne suis pas un héros. Je suis un être humain." »
Mary Astor

Orchid (1940), il joue les seconds couteaux aux côtés de James Cagney ou d'Edward. G. Robinson. Bogart se bat alors bec et ongles contre la Warner, à l'instar d'autres «larbins asservis» (selon ses propres termes) tels que Bette Davis.

Pendant ce temps, sa vie privée tourne au chaos. Toujours attiré par les femmes fortes et agressives à l'image de sa mère, il a fort à faire avec sa troisième épouse, l'actrice Mayo Methot. Bien que tous deux boivent abondamment, se disputent violemment et s'aiment passionnément, ils exercent une influence positive sur leurs carrières respectives. Bogart suit les conseils de son épouse, qui l'encourage à se battre pour obtenir des rôles plus intéressants. Leur persévérance est récompensée lorsqu'il décroche le rôle du gangster vieillissant Roy Earle dans *La Grande Évasion* (1941), qui a été refusé par Paul Muni et George Raft. Le succès critique et commercial du film lui ouvre la voie de deux autres rôles marquants. Le premier est celui du détective Sam Spade dans *Le Faucon maltais* (1941) de John Huston, inspiré d'un roman de Dashiell Hammett. Le second, le plus célèbre de tous, est celui de Rick Blaine, l'expatrié désabusé de *Casablanca* (1942). Avec ces trois rôles majeurs, Bogart affine son personnage à la fois dur à cuire et torturé, définissant l'archétype du héros de film noir des années 1940.

Jusqu'à la fin de sa carrière, Bogart continuera à peaufiner son image ténébreuse. Il aura souvent pour partenaire la dernière et la plus célèbre de ses épouses, l'actrice et mannequin Lauren Bacall, une autre femme de tête. Ensemble, ils tourneront trois classiques du film noir, *Le Port de l'angoisse* (1944), *Le Grand Sommeil* (1946) et *Les Passagers de la nuit* (1947). Ils défileront également à la tête d'un cortège de personnalités du cinéma protestant contre la «chasse aux sorcières» du sénateur McCarthy et de la Commission parlementaire sur les activités anti-américaines. Malgré la controverse suscitée au sein d'une industrie cinématographique terrifiée, de tels actes de bravoure contribueront à faire de Bogart un mythe, celui de l'iconoclaste défenseur des opprimés.

En 1952, son statut de mythe et ses talents d'acteurs sont enfin reconnus par ses pairs, qui lui décernent un Oscar pour son rôle dans *L'Odyssée de l'African Queen* (1951) de John Huston. Il reçoit également des critiques dithyrambiques pour son interprétation de Queeg, le commandant psychotique d'*Ouragan sur le Caine* (1954). Bien que Bogart succombe à un cancer en 1957, ces films achèvent d'asseoir sa légende. Désormais immortel, le mythe Bogart est entré dans l'histoire.

PAGE 22
PORTRAIT (1930)
The young, handsome Bogie, a demeanor that would land him mostly "fluff" theater roles. / Sein gutes Aussehen brachte dem jungen Bogie vor allem „belanglose" Bühnenrollen ein. / L'allure de jeune premier qui le cantonnera dans des rôles «légers» au théâtre.

PORTRAIT FOR 'IN A LONELY PLACE' (1950)
Bogart gives one of his most complex performances on male violence. / Bogart in einer seiner vielschichtigsten Darstellungen zum Thema männliche Gewalt. / Bogart dans l'une de ses représentations les plus complexes de la violence masculine.

2

VISUAL FILMOGRAPHY

FILMOGRAFIE IN BILDERN
FILMOGRAPHIE EN IMAGES

EARLY DAYS

ANFANGSJAHRE

LES DÉBUTS

FROM THE PLAY 'HELL'S BELLS' (1925)
Bogart emotes in a play deemed 'painfully synthetic' by
the critics. / Bogart zeigt Gefühle in einem Stück, das
Kritiker als „schmerzhaft gekünstelt" bezeichneten. /
Rôle sentimental dans une pièce jugée
« douloureusement artificielle » par la critique.

FROM THE PLAY 'NERVES' (1924)
Bogart romances his future wife Mary Philips. / Bogart
umschwärmt seine künftige Ehefrau Mary Philips. /
Dans les bras de sa future épouse, Mary Philips.

FROM THE PLAY 'IT'S A WISE CHILD' (1929)
Although this romantic comedy was a hit, Bogart
wanted to try Hollywood. / Obwohl diese
Liebeskomödie ein Erfolg war, wollte Bogart sein Glück
in Hollywood versuchen. / Malgré le succès de cette
comédie romantique, Bogart veut tenter sa chance à
Hollywood.

"I'm not at ease with women, really. I must
obviously like certain women. I've certainly married
enough of them."
Humphrey Bogart

„Ich fühle mich in der Nähe von Frauen unwohl,
wirklich. Offensichtlich mag ich bestimmte Frauen.
Jedenfalls habe ich genug von ihnen geheiratet."
Humphrey Bogart

« En fait, je ne suis pas très à l'aise avec les
femmes. Mais il y en a manifestement qui me
plaisent. Il suffit de voir combien j'en ai épousé. »
Humphrey Bogart

STILL FROM 'BROADWAY'S LIKE THAT' (1930)
An early Vitaphone short with star Ruth Etting, filmed in
New York. / Ein früher Kurzfilm, den Vitaphone in New
York drehte, mit Ruth Etting in der Hauptrolle. / Court
métrage tourné à New York à l'aide du Vitaphone, aux
côtés de la star Ruth Etting.

STILL FROM 'A DEVIL WITH WOMEN' (1930)
In Hollywood, Bogart still played a spoiled son of the
upper-class ... but with a rifle. / Auch in Hollywood
spielte Bogart noch immer den verwöhnten Sohn aus
gutem Hause, aber diesmal mit einem Gewehr in der
Hand. / À Hollywood, Bogart incarne encore un fils de
bonne famille ... mais armé d'un fusil.

STILL FROM 'UP THE RIVER' (1930)
A lifelong friendship with fellow hard-living actor
Spencer Tracy was cemented on this film. / Bei diesem
Film entstand eine lebenslange Freundschaft mit
seinem Kollegen Spencer Tracy, der wie er sein Dasein
in vollen Zügen auslebte. / Ce film scelle une longue
amitié avec un autre bon vivant, l'acteur Spencer Tracy.

STILL FROM 'BAD SISTER' (1931)
Bogart darkens his image a little as a con man and
works with fellow rebel Bette Davis (seated). / Bogart
verdüstert sein Image als Gauner noch ein wenig und
arbeitet mit seiner ebenso aufsässigen Kollegin Bette
Davis (sitzend) zusammen. / Bogart assombrit un peu
son image en incarnant un escroc aux côtés d'une autre
rebelle, Bette Davis (assise).

STILL FROM 'BODY AND SOUL' (1931)
Bogart is killed off in this military movie. His buddies are
Charles Farrell and Don Dillaway. / In diesem Militärfilm
wird Bogarts Figur getötet. Seine Kameraden werden
von Charles Farrell und Don Dillaway gespielt. / Entouré
ici de ses camarades (Charles Farrell et Don Dillaway),
Jim (Bogart) trouvera la mort dans ce film de guerre.

PAGES 32/33
STILL FROM 'LOVE AFFAIR' (1932)
Films like this melodrama with Dorothy MacKaill made
Bogart despair, so he returned to Broadway. / Filme wie
dieses Melodrama mit Dorothy MacKaill trieben Bogart
zur Verzweiflung und veranlassten ihn zur Rückkehr an
den Broadway. / Découragé par des films tels que ce
mélodrame avec Dorothy MacKaill, Bogart retourne à
Broadway.

PAGE 34
STILL FROM 'BULLETS OR BALLOTS' (1936)
Bogart comes into his own as the psychologically
scarred heavy. / Als psychisch angeschlagener
Bösewicht etabliert Bogart seinen eigenen Typus. /
Bogart montre de quoi il est capable dans un rôle de
truand marqué psychologiquement.

THE HEAVY

SCHURKENSTÜCKE

LE TRUAND

FROM THE PLAY 'THE PETRIFIED FOREST' (1935)

Bogart rehearses on stage in his first breakthrough role as Duke Mantee. / Bogart probt auf der Bühne für seinen ersten Durchbruch in der Rolle des Duke Mantee. / Répétition théâtrale avec Bogart dans le rôle de Duke Mantee, le premier à l'avoir révélé.

"My best shot was Leslie Howard in 'The Petrified Forest.' I got him with one bullet and he died quick. The others have been slow bleeders and most of the time they lived long enough to kill me."
Humphrey Bogart

„Mein bester Schuss war der auf Leslie Howard in Der versteinerte Wald. Ich hab ihn mit einer einzigen Kugel erwischt, und er ist schnell gestorben. Die anderen sind langsam verblutet und waren meist noch lange genug am Leben, um mich zu töten."
Humphrey Bogart

« Mon meilleur tir, c'est sur Leslie Howard dans La Forêt pétrifiée. Je l'ai eu d'une seule balle et il est mort rapidement. Les autres saignaient à n'en plus finir et survivaient généralement assez longtemps pour me tuer. »
Humphrey Bogart

STILL FROM 'THE PETRIFIED FOREST' (1936)
Leslie Howard (on floor with Bette Davis) insisted that
Bogart play Mantee in the film. / Leslie Howard (am
Boden neben Bette Davis) bestand darauf, dass Bogart
auch in der Verfilmung Mantee spielen durfte. / Leslie
Howard (par terre avec Bette Davis) a insisté pour que
Bogart joue Mantee dans l'adaptation cinémato-
graphique.

PAGES 38/39
STILL FROM 'BULLETS OR BALLOTS' (1936)
Warner Brothers immediately cast Bogart as another
gangster after the success of 'The Petrified Forest.' /
Nach dem Erfolg von *Der versteinerte Wald* gab Warner
Bros. Bogart sofort wieder eine Gangsterrolle. / Après
le succès de *La Forêt pétrifiée*, la Warner confie
immédiatement à Bogart un autre rôle de gangster.

STILL FROM 'CHINA CLIPPER' (1936)
Warners continued to misuse Bogart's talent. Here he
plays flying ace Hap Stuart ... / Warner Bros. verheizte
Bogarts Talent weiter. Hier spielt er das Fliegeras Hap
Stuart ... / La Warner continue à gâcher le talent de
Bogart, qui incarne ici l'as des airs Hap Stuart ...

"Do you realize you're looking at an actor who's
made more lousy pictures than any other in
history."
Humphrey Bogart

„Ist Ihnen klar, dass Sie einen Schauspieler vor sich
sehen, der mehr lausige Filme gedreht hat als
irgendein anderer in der Geschichte?"
Humphrey Bogart

« Vous avez devant vous l'acteur qui a tourné le
plus grand nombre de navets dans l'histoire du
cinéma. »
Humphrey Bogart

STILL FROM 'ISLE OF FURY' (1936)
... and this one features a shipwreck and a huge
octopus. / ... und hier geht es um ein Schiffsunglück und
einen Riesenkraken. / ... et affronte ici un naufrage et
une pieuvre géante.

STILL FROM 'BLACK LEGION' (1937)
In his first leading role, Bogart was supported by Helen
Flint and Joe Sawyer. / In seiner ersten Hauptrolle
standen Bogart Helen Flint und Joe Sawyer zur Seite. /
Pour ses débuts dans un premier rôle, Bogart est
entouré de Helen Flint et Joe Sawyer.

PORTRAIT FOR 'BLACK LEGION' (1937)
Both Bogart and the public reacted well to this socially
conscious film about American racism. / Sowohl Bogart
als auch das Publikum zeigten sich angetan von diesem
sozialkritischen Film über Rassismus in den USA. /
L'acteur et le public réagissent bien à ce film social sur
le racisme américain.

STILL FROM 'MARKED WOMAN' (1937)
A role Bogart fought for, the chance to play the heroic
district attorney David Graham. / Bogart kämpfte hart
darum, den heldenhaften Staatsanwalt David Graham
spielen zu dürfen. / Un rôle pour lequel Bogart s'est
battu, celui de l'héroïque procureur David Graham.

PORTRAIT FOR 'MARKED WOMAN' (1937)
Bogart also got to work again with friend and fellow
studio rebel Bette Davis. / Wieder einmal konnte
Bogart an der Seite seiner guten Freundin Bette Davis
spielen, die in den Studios als ebenso rebellisch galt wie
er. / Il y retrouve une autre rebelle aux prises avec la
Warner, son amie Bette Davis.

STILL FROM 'KID GALAHAD' (1937)
Bogart battles Edward G. Robinson and Bette Davis for
control of a fighter. / Bogart kämpft mit Edward G.
Robinson und Bette Davis um die Kontrolle über einen
Boxer. / Bogart tente d'arracher un boxeur à Edward G.
Robinson et à Bette Davis.

"All you owe the public is a good performance."
Humphrey Bogart

*„Alles, was man dem Publikum schuldet, ist eine
gute schauspielerische Leistung."*
Humphrey Bogart

*« Tout ce qu'on doit au public, c'est une bonne
prestation. »*
Humphrey Bogart

STILL FROM 'SAN QUENTIN' (1937)
Stock Warners prison drama with Bogart as Joe "Red"
Kennedy. / Ein Gefängnisdrama von der Stange für
Warner Bros. mit Bogart in der Rolle des Joe „Red"
Kennedy. / Drame derrière les barreaux, avec Bogart
dans le rôle de « Red ».

PAGES 48/49
ON THE SET OF 'DEAD END' (1937)
Illustrious director William Wyler directs Bogart in one
of his finest roles, gangster "Baby Face" Martin. / Unter
der Regie des berühmten William Wyler spielte Bogart
eine seiner besten Rollen: die des Gangsters „Baby
Face" Martin. / L'illustre réalisateur William Wyler dirige
Bogart dans l'un de ses meilleurs rôles, celui du gangster
« Baby Face » Martin.

STILL FROM 'DEAD END' (1937)
His mother (Marjorie Main) rejects him because
of his criminal ways. / Wegen seiner kriminellen
Machenschaften wird er von seiner Mutter (Marjorie
Main) zurückgewiesen. / La mère (Marjorie Main)
rejette son fils devenu gangster.

*"It takes a long time to develop a repulsive
character like mine."*
Humphrey Bogart

*„Es dauert lange, bis man eine so widerwärtige
Figur wie meine entwickelt hat."*
Humphrey Bogart

*« Il faut du temps pour mettre au point un
personnage aussi repoussant que le mien. »*
Humphrey Bogart

STILL FROM 'DEAD END' (1937)
"Baby Face" registers the kind of angst Bogart was
soon to become famous for. / „Baby Face" zeigte
bereits jene Existenzangst, die für Bogart bald darauf
zum Markenzeichen wurde. / « Baby Face » en proie à
l'angoisse existentielle pour laquelle Bogart deviendra
bientôt célèbre.

STILL FROM 'DEAD END' (1937)
His "girl" (Claire Trevor) has fallen into prostitution and
is suffering from a fatal disease. / Seine „Braut" (Claire
Trevor) ist in die Prostitution abgeglitten und hat sich
eine tödliche Krankheit zugezogen. / Sa « fiancée »
(Claire Trevor) a sombré dans la prostitution et souffre
d'une maladie mortelle.

ON THE SET OF 'DEAD END' (1937)
Again Bogart hoped that his outstanding performance
would merit better roles. It was not to be. / Wieder
einmal hoffte Bogart, dass ihm seine ausgezeichnete
schauspielerische Leistung bessere Rollen einbrächte,
doch es sollte nicht sein. / Espérant que son jeu
admirable lui vaudrait de meilleurs rôles, Bogart sera
à nouveau déçu.

STILL FROM 'STAND-IN' (1937)
Working again with friend and mentor Leslie Howard. /
Wieder konnte er mit seinem Freund und Mentor Leslie
Howard zusammenarbeiten. / Nouvelle collaboration
avec son ami et mentor Leslie Howard.

ON THE SET OF 'STAND-IN' (1937)
Bogart, like many actors, had a small dressing room and
wore his own clothes onscreen. / Bogart hatte, wie viele
Schauspieler, nur eine kleine Garderobe und trug im
Film seine eigene Kleidung. / Comme beaucoup
d'acteurs, Bogart possède une petite loge et porte ses
propres vêtements à l'écran.

STILL FROM 'SWING YOUR LADY' (1938)
This Ozarks comedy was one of the many reasons for
Bogart's growing disillusionment with Warners. / Diese
Komödie, die in den Ozarks spielt, war einer von vielen
Gründen für Bogarts wachsende Enttäuschung über
Warner Bros. / Cette comédie burlesque tournée dans
les Ozarks, au fin fond du Missouri, est l'une des
nombreuses raisons qui poussent Bogart à désespérer
de la Warner.

*"The only true test [of acting ability] would be to
have every actor play Hamlet and decide who is
best."*
Humphrey Bogart

*„Der einzig wahre Test schauspielerischer
Fähigkeiten wäre es, jeden Schauspieler Hamlet
spielen zu lassen und dann zu entscheiden, wer der
Beste ist."*
Humphrey Bogart

*« Le seul véritable test [du talent d'acteur] serait de
faire jouer Hamlet à chaque comédien pour
décider qui est le meilleur. »*
Humphrey Bogart

STILL FROM 'CRIME SCHOOL' (1938)
Bogart teams up again with the 'Dead End' kids, but
without a dynamic script and director. / Bogart steht
wieder mit den Jungen aus *Sackgasse* vor der Kamera,
aber diesmal fehlen dem Drehbuch und Regisseur die
Dynamik. / Bogart retrouve les gamins de *Rue sans
issue*, avec un scénario et un réalisateur hélas moins
dynamiques.

PORTRAIT (1936)
Bogart 'projects' the image of a 'classic' actor, again for
the benefit of the publicity department at Warners. /
Bogart soll das Image eines „klassischen" Schauspielers
„vermitteln" – auch hier wieder für die Werbeabteilung
von Warner Bros. / Bogart « projette » l'image d'un
acteur « classique », là encore pour le compte du
service marketing de la Warner.

PORTRAIT (1939)
The silly things publicity departments ask artists to do
and put up with. / Ein Beispiel für den Schwachsinn,
den sich die Werbeabteilungen einfallen ließen und die
Künstler ertragen mussten. / Le genre d'inepties que les
services marketing font subir aux artistes.

ON THE SET OF 'MEN ARE SUCH FOOLS' (1938)

Bogart and Hugh Herbert take a break from making another fluff movie to photograph Priscilla Lane. / Während einer Drehpause für einen weiteren belanglosen Streifen fotografieren Bogart und Hugh Herbert ihre Kollegin Priscilla Lane. / Bogart et Hugh Herbert photographient Priscilla Lane pendant le tournage d'une nouvelle comédie légère.

"I was born indolent and this [acting] was the softest of rackets."
Humphrey Bogart

„Ich bin von Geburt aus faul, und die Schauspielerei war der bequemste aller Berufe."
Humphrey Bogart

« Je suis d'un naturel indolent et ceci [le métier d'acteur] était la plus douce des escroqueries. »
Humphrey Bogart

ON THE SET OF 'THE AMAZING DR. CLITTERHOUSE' (1938)
Bogart resented being second-billed to tough guys like
Edward G. Robinson, James Cagney and George Raft. /
Bogart störte es, dass er stets an zweiter Stelle genannt
wurde – nach den Darstellern harter Burschen wie
Edward G. Robinson, James Cagney und George Raft. /
Bogart frustré de jouer les seconds rôles aux côtés
d'Edward G. Robinson, James Cagney ou George Raft.

ADVERT FOR 'RACKET BUSTERS' (1938)

PORTRAIT FOR 'RACKET BUSTERS' (1938)
A mediocre gangster film at the end of the
gangster cycle with Bogart as John "Czar" Martin. /
Ein mittelmäßiger Gangsterfilm am Ende des
Gangsterzyklus mit Bogart als John „Czar" Martin. /
Film médiocre où Bogart incarne le gangster John
Martin, alias « Czar ».

**STILL FROM 'ANGELS WITH DIRTY FACES'
(1938)**
As crooked lawyer James Frazier, Bogart is buried
by the expressionistic performance of star James
Cagney. / In der Rolle des korrupten Rechtsanwalts
James Frazier wird Bogarts Leistung von James
Cagneys expressionistischer Darstellung in den
Schatten gestellt. / Dans le rôle de l'avocat véreux
James Frazier, Bogart est éclipsé par le jeu
expressionniste de James Cagney.

"You're not a star until they can spell your name in
Karachi."
Humphrey Bogart

„Du bist erst dann ein Star, wenn sie deinen Namen
auch in Karatschi buchstabieren können."
Humphrey Bogart

« Vous n'êtes pas une star tant qu'on ne sait pas
écrire votre nom à Karachi. »
Humphrey Bogart

**STILL FROM 'ANGELS WITH DIRTY FACES'
(1938)**
Frazier betrays his client, but he will pay for it. / Frazier
muss dafür büßen, dass er seinen Klienten hintergeht. /
La trahison de son client va coûter cher à Frazier.

Jail breaker of "San Quentin"

Killer of "Dr. Clitterhou[se]"

Mobster of "Kid Galahad"

Super-Gangster o[f] "Racket Busters[]"

**STILL FROM 'KING OF THE UNDERWORLD'
(1939)**
Gangster Joe Gurney gets his eyes checked by
compassionate doctor Carole Nelson (Kay Francis). /
Der Gangster Joe Gurney lässt sich von der
mitleidsvollen Ärztin Carole Nelson (Kay Francis) die
Augen untersuchen. / Le gangster Joe Gurney se fait
examiner par le docteur Carole Nelson (Kay Francis).

**ADVERT FOR 'KING OF THE UNDERWORLD'
(1939)**
Exploiting Bogart's gangster image. / Hier schlägt man
Kapital aus Bogarts Gangsterimage. / Exploitation de
l'image de gangster de Bogart.

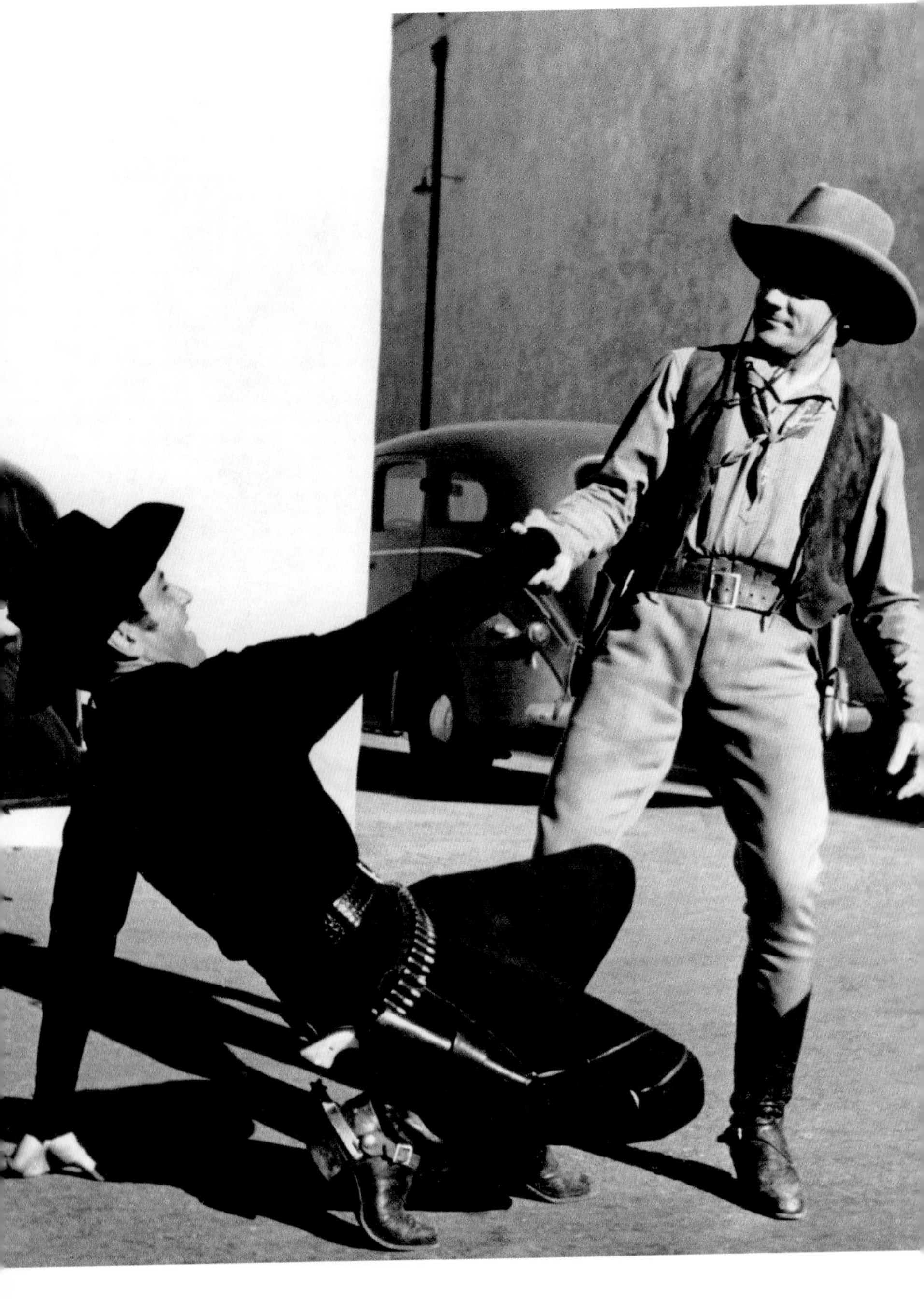

STILL FROM 'VIRGINIA CITY' (1940)
Bogart's 'swarthy' looks and a fake mustache enhance his villainous image. / Bogarts „dunkles" Erscheinungsbild und ein falscher Schnurrbart verstärken sein Bild als Bösewicht. / Son air « basané » et sa fausse moustache accentuent son allure de bandit.

ON THE SET OF 'THE OKLAHOMA KID' (1939)
Bogart plays second fiddle again. He even needs James Cagney's help to get up. / Bogart spielt schon wieder die zweite Geige. Sogar zum Aufstehen ist er auf die Hilfe von James Cagney angewiesen. / Éternel second rôle, Bogart a besoin de James Cagney pour l'aider à se relever.

ON THE SET OF 'DARK VICTORY' (1939)
Bogart as Michael O' Leary, terribly miscast as Bette
Davis' Irish stable foreman. / Bogart als Michael
O'Leary, fürchterlich fehlbesetzt als der irische
Stallmeister von Judith Traherne (Bette Davis). / Bogart
terriblement à contre-emploi en dresseur de chevaux
irlandais employé par Bette Davis.

STILL FROM 'DARK VICTORY' (1939)
But at least he was not playing a one-dimensional
villain. / Wenigstens spielte er keinen farblosen
Schurken. / Un rôle qui le change des personnages de
méchants caricaturaux …

This Man
Will Kill – and
Be Killed!

STILL FROM 'THE ROARING TWENTIES' (1939)
This Raoul Walsh-directed film is far better than most.
It is an elegy to the gangster film cycle now at its official
end. / Dieser Film unter der Regie von Raoul Walsh war
weitaus besser als die meisten anderen. Er ist der
Abgesang auf den Zyklus von Gangsterfilmen, der nun
ganz offiziell am Ende ist. / Bien supérieur à la moyenne,
ce film de Raoul Walsh est une ode aux histoires de
gangster, dont l'âge d'or est officiellement terminé.

**ADVERT FOR 'YOU CAN'T GET AWAY WITH
MURDER' (1939)**
As Frank Wilson in yet another Warners cheapie. /
Als Frank Wilson in einer weiteren Billigproduktion für
Warner Bros. / Dans le rôle de Frank Wilson pour une
autre série B de la Warner.

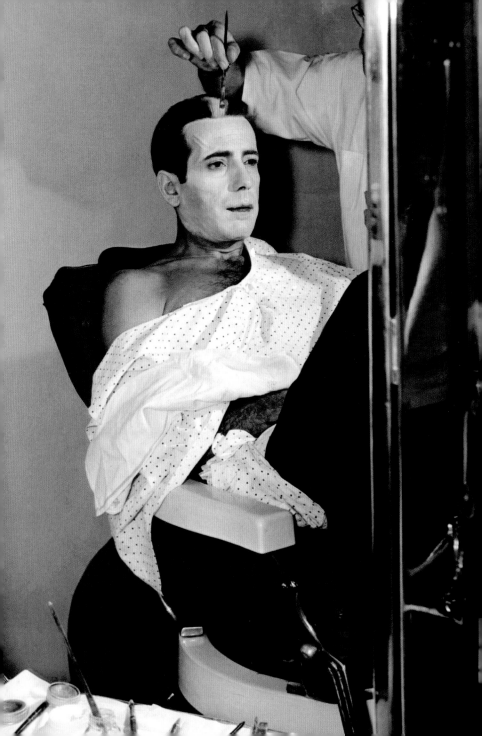

STILL FROM 'THE RETURN OF DR. X' (1939)
Bogart dies in most of his Warners films, allowing him to move directly onto the set of his next film. / In den meisten Filmen für Warner Bros. stirbt Bogart und hat so die Möglichkeit, gleich zu seinem nächsten Film überzugehen. / Bogart meurt dans la plupart des films de la Warner, ce qui lui permet d'enchaîner rapidement les tournages.

ON THE SET OF 'THE RETURN OF DR. X' (1939)
Having his make-up applied. / In der Maske. / Séance de maquillage.

PAGES 76/77
ON THE SET OF 'INVISIBLE STRIPES' (1939)
This prison shower scene with George Raft was quite risqué for its time. / Diese Szene im Duschraum des Gefängnisses war für ihre Zeit recht gewagt. / Cette scène, où Bogart prisonnier se douche aux côtés de George Raft, est assez osée pour l'époque.

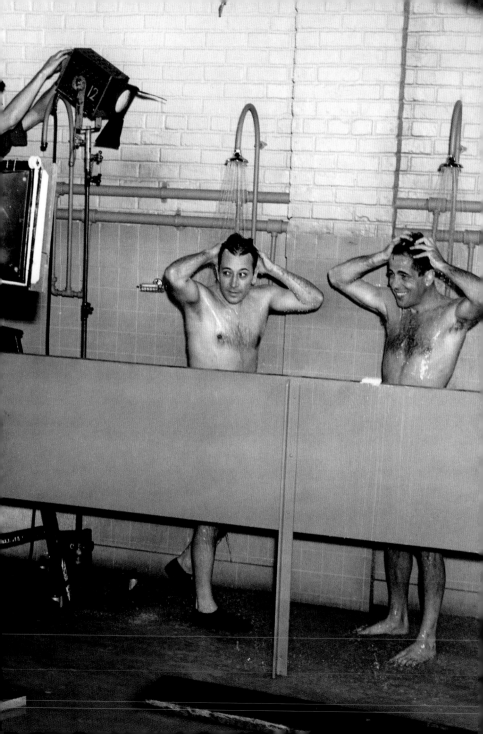

STILL FROM 'IT ALL CAME TRUE' (1940)
Gangster Grasselli is forcefed by Maggie and Norah as he hides out from the law. / Der Gangster Grasselli wird von Maggie und Norah zwangsernährt, während er sich vor der Polizei versteckt. / Grasselli, gangster en cavale, est nourri de force par Maggie et Norah.

"You know, I think I owe my career to Clark Gable. He was a pioneer. Once it was found that women raved over him, big ears and all, the way was cleared for all us ugly mugs."
Humphrey Bogart

„Wissen Sie, ich glaube, ich verdanke meine Karriere Clark Gable. Er war ein Pionier. Als man festgestellt hatte, dass die Frauen bei diesem Typen mit seinen Riesenohren und alldem ins Schwärmen gerieten, da war die Bahn frei für hässliche Visagen wie meine."
Humphrey Bogart

« Vous savez, je crois que je dois ma carrière à Clark Gable. C'était un pionnier. Une fois qu'on a découvert que les femmes étaient folles de lui avec ses grandes oreilles, il a ouvert la voie à toutes les salles gueules comme la mienne. »
Humphrey Bogart

ON THE SET OF 'BROTHER ORCHID' (1940)
A classic gangster comedy which rips apart the
conventions of the genre. / Eine klassische
Gangsterkomödie, die die Konventionen des Genres in
Stücke reißt. / Une comédie de gangsters qui met à mal
les conventions du genre.

STILL FROM 'THEY DRIVE BY NIGHT' (1940)
Bogart registers a powerful performance as working-class trucker struggling to survive. / Bogart gibt eine eindrucksvolle darstellerische Leistung als Lkw-Fahrer, der ums Überleben kämpft. / Puissante interprétation de Bogart en camionneur luttant pour sa survie.

PORTRAIT
Bicycle: a common form of transportation around Warner's studio. / Das Fahrrad war ein verbreitetes Fortbewegungsmittel auf dem Studiogelände der Warner Bros. / Le vélo, moyen de transport courant dans les studios de la Warner.

PAGE 82
PORTRAIT FOR 'HIGH SIERRA' (1941)
With the help of wife Mayo Methot, Bogart finally captures the role of a lifetime. / Mit Unterstützung seiner Ehefrau Mayo Methot ergattert Bogart endlich die Rolle seines Lebens. / Avec l'aide de son épouse Mayo Methot, Bogart décroche enfin le rôle de sa vie.

LEADING MAN

HAUPTROLLEN

LA STAR

ON THE SET OF 'HIGH SIERRA' (1941)
Director Raoul Walsh runs actors Henry Travers and
Bogart through their lines. / Regisseur Raoul Walsh geht
mit den Schauspielern Henry Travers und Humphrey
Bogart den Text durch. / Le réalisateur Raoul Walsh fait
répéter Henry Travers et Humphrey Bogart.

PORTRAIT FOR 'HIGH SIERRA' (1941)
Bogart's performance as "Mad Dog" Earle transforms
his career and shapes the noir anti-hero. / Bogarts
schauspielerische Leistung als „Mad Dog" Earle gibt
seiner Karriere eine neue Richtung und dem Antihelden
des *Film noir* eine Vorlage. / Son interprétation du
personnage de Roy Earle transforme sa carrière et
donne naissance à l'antihéros de film noir.

STILL FROM 'HIGH SIERRA' (1941)
The fatherly gangster with his young lover and admirer
Marie Garson (Ida Lupino). / Der väterliche Gangster
mit seiner jungen Geliebten und Bewunderin Marie
Garson (Ida Lupino). / Le gangster paternel et sa jeune
maîtresse et admiratrice Marie Garson (Ida Lupino).

"I wouldn't give you two cents for a dame without a
temper."
Roy Earle, 'High Sierra' (1941)

„Ich würde dir keine zwei Cents geben für eine
Puppe ohne Temperament."
Roy Earle, Entscheidung in der Sierra (1941)

« Je ne donnerais pas deux sous pour une dame
sans tempérament. »
Roy Earle, La Grande Évasion (1941)

STILL FROM 'HIGH SIERRA' (1941)
Pursued and isolated in the mountains, the classic
noir protagonist fights back. / Verfolgt und in die
Abgeschiedenheit der Berge getrieben, setzt sich der
klassische Protagonist des Film noir zur Wehr. /
Pourchassé et isolé dans la montagne, le héros solitaire
contre-attaque.

**STILL FROM 'THE WAGONS ROLL AT NIGHT'
(1941)**
Although this film was no challenge for Bogart, it made
more money than 'The Maltese Falcon.' / Obwohl der
Film für Bogart keine Herausforderung war, brachte er
ihm mehr Geld ein als *Die Spur des Falken*. / Bien que
ce film n'ait guère marqué sa carrière, il rapporte plus
d'argent que *Le Faucon maltais*.

"I would have liked to be anything but an actor. It's
such a stupid thing to be."
Humphrey Bogart

„Ich wäre gern alles andere gewesen, nur kein
Schauspieler. Das ist so ein bescheuerter Beruf."
Humphrey Bogart

« J'aurais aimé être n'importe quoi, sauf acteur.
C'est un métier tellement idiot. »
Humphrey Bogart

**STILL FROM 'THE WAGONS ROLL AT NIGHT'
(1941)**
Bogart wants to protect his "pure" sister Mary (Joan
Leslie) from suitor Matt Varney (Eddie Albert). / Bogart
möchte seine „unschuldige" Schwester Mary (Joan
Leslie) vor ihrem Freier Matt Varney (Eddie Albert)
schützen. / Bogart protège la « pureté » de sa sœur
Mary (Joan Leslie) contre les avances de Matt Varney
(Eddie Albert).

"Physically, I'm not tough. I may think tough.
I would say I'm kinda tough and calloused inside.
I could use a foot more in height and fifty more
pounds and fifteen years off my age and then God
help all you bastards."
Humphrey Bogart

„Körperlich bin ich kein harter Burscher – in
Gedanken vielleicht. Ich würde sagen, innerlich bin
ich irgendwie abgehärtet. Wenn ich einen Fuß
größer wäre und fünfzig Pfund schwerer und
fünfzehn Jahre jünger, dann – Gnade euch Gott,
ihr Bastarde!"
Humphrey Bogart

« Physiquement, je ne suis pas un dur. Je peux
être dur mentalement. Je dirais que je suis dur
et insensible à l'intérieur. Si je faisais trente
centimètres et vingt-cinq kilos de plus et si j'avais
quinze ans de moins, les salauds n'auraient qu'à
bien se tenir. »
Humphrey Bogart

"Bogart can be a tough guy without a gun. Also he
has a sense of humor that contains the grating
undertone of contempt."
Raymond Chandler, writer

„Bogart kann ohne Waffe hart sein. Außerdem
besitzt er einen Sinn für Humor mit dem
knirschenden Unterton der Verachtung."
Raymond Chandler, Schriftsteller

« Bogart peut être un dur sans revolver. Il possède
également un sens de l'humour qui contient une
note de mépris grinçant. »
Raymond Chandler, écrivain

**PORTRAIT FOR 'THE MALTESE FALCON'
(1941)**
For generations to come, Bogart incarnates Dashiell
Hammett's noir detective Sam Spade. / Auch für
nachfolgende Generationen blieb Bogart vor allem die
Inkarnation von Dashiell Hammetts Film-noir-Detektiv
Sam Spade. / Pour toutes les générations à venir, Bogart
incarnera le détective Sam Spade créé par Dashiell
Hammett.

PAGES 92/93
STILL FROM 'THE MALTESE FALCON' (1941)
The brilliant ensemble cast (left to right: Bogart, Peter
Lorre, Mary Astor, and Sydney Greenstreet) holds "the
stuff that dreams are made of." / Das glänzende
Schauspielerensemble (von links nach rechts: Bogart,
Peter Lorre, Mary Astor und Sydney Greenstreet) hält
„den Stoff, aus dem Träume sind" in Händen. / Un
prestigieux casting (de gauche à droite : Bogart, Peter
Lorre, Mary Astor et Sydney Greenstreet) fasciné par
l'objet de tous les désirs.

STILL FROM 'THE MALTESE FALCON' (1941)
Hardboiled ethics even include the woman you love.
Bogart threatens the duplicitous Brigid (Mary Astor). /
Die Ethik der „Hartgesottenen" macht auch vor der
Frau, die man liebt, nicht Halt. Sam (Bogart) droht Brigid
(Mary Astor), die ein doppeltes Spiel treibt. / Une
morale implacable s'applique aussi à la femme qu'on
aime. Bogart menace la fourbe Brigid (Mary Astor).

"I'll be waiting for you. If they hang you, I'll always
remember you."
Sam Spade to Brigid, 'The Maltese Falcon' (1941)

„Ich werde auf dich warten. Wenn sie dich
aufhängen, werde ich dich in guter Erinnerung
behalten."
Sam Spade zu Brigid, Die Spur des Falken (1941)

« Je t'attendrai. S'ils te pendent, je ne t'oublierai
jamais. »
Sam Spade à Brigid, Le Faucon maltais (1941)

STILL FROM 'THE MALTESE FALCON' (1941)
A more romantic moment between the noir couple. /
Ein etwas romantischerer Augenblick zwischen dem
Film-noir-Pärchen. / Scène plus romantique entre les
amants maudits.

**STILL FROM 'ALL THROUGH THE NIGHT'
(1942)**
As a veteran of World War One, Bogart was forced to
battle World War Two onscreen. / Bogart, der selbst ein
Veteran des Ersten Weltkriegs war, kämpfte auf der
Leinwand im Zweiten. / Vétéran de la Première Guerre
mondiale, Bogart combat dans la Seconde à l'écran.

"I'd never hit a lady, they're too dangerous."
Humphrey Bogart

*„Ich würde nie eine Dame schlagen. Die sind zu
gefährlich."*
Humphrey Bogart

*« Je ne frapperais jamais une femme, elles sont
trop dangereuses. »*
Humphrey Bogart

STILL FROM 'THE BIG SHOT' (1942)
Bogart brings the emotional baggage from 'High Sierra'
to his portrayal of another aging convict. / Bogart bringt
die Gefühlswelt aus *Entscheidung in der Sierra* in die
Darstellung eines weiteren alternden Sträflings ein. /
Bogart apporte le bagage émotionnel de *La Grande
Évasion* dans ce portrait d'un autre prisonnier
vieillissant.

PAGES 98/99
STILL FROM 'ACROSS THE PACIFIC' (1942)
Bogart reunites with director John Huston and Mary
Astor (under pillow) to fight the war. / Bogart arbeitet
in diesem Kriegsstreifen wieder mit Regisseur John
Huston und mit Mary Astor (unter dem Kissen)
zusammen. / Bogart retrouve le réalisateur John Huston
et sa partenaire Mary Astor (sous l'oreiller) dans un film
de guerre.

STILL FROM 'CASABLANCA' (1942)
Bogart projects the wounded, vulnerable quality that endeared him to audiences. Peter Lorre watches curiously. / Bogart zeigt jene Verletztheit und Verwundbarkeit, die das Publikum an ihm so sehr schätzte. Peter Lorre beobachtet ihn interessiert. / Bogart arbore l'air blessé et vulnérable qui lui attire la sympathie du public, sous le regard intrigué de Peter Lorre.

PORTRAIT FOR 'CASABLANCA' (1942)
The film that did more to help Bogart keep his iconic status through the decades. / Dieser Film trug über die Jahrzehnte wohl am meisten dazu bei, dass Bogart seinen Status als Ikone aufrechterhalten konnte. / Le film qui contribuera le plus au mythe Bogart au fil des décennies.

STILL FROM 'CASABLANCA' (1942)
Everyone has an angle in Casablanca. Here Sydney
Greenstreet tries one on the alienated Bogart. /
In Casablanca verfolgt jeder ein bestimmtes Ziel. Hier
versucht Ferrari (Sydney Greenstreet) sein Glück bei
einem missmutigen Rick (Bogart). / À Casablanca,
chacun a son point de vue. Sydney Greenstreet tente
d'imposer le sien à un Bogart désabusé.

ON THE SET OF 'CASABLANCA' (1942)
Bogart and Ingrid Bergman in the idyllic flashback to
happier times in Paris. / Bogart und Ingrid Bergman in
der idyllischen Rückblende auf glücklichere Zeiten in
Paris. / Bogart et Ingrid Bergman dans le flash-back
rappelant leur idylle à Paris.

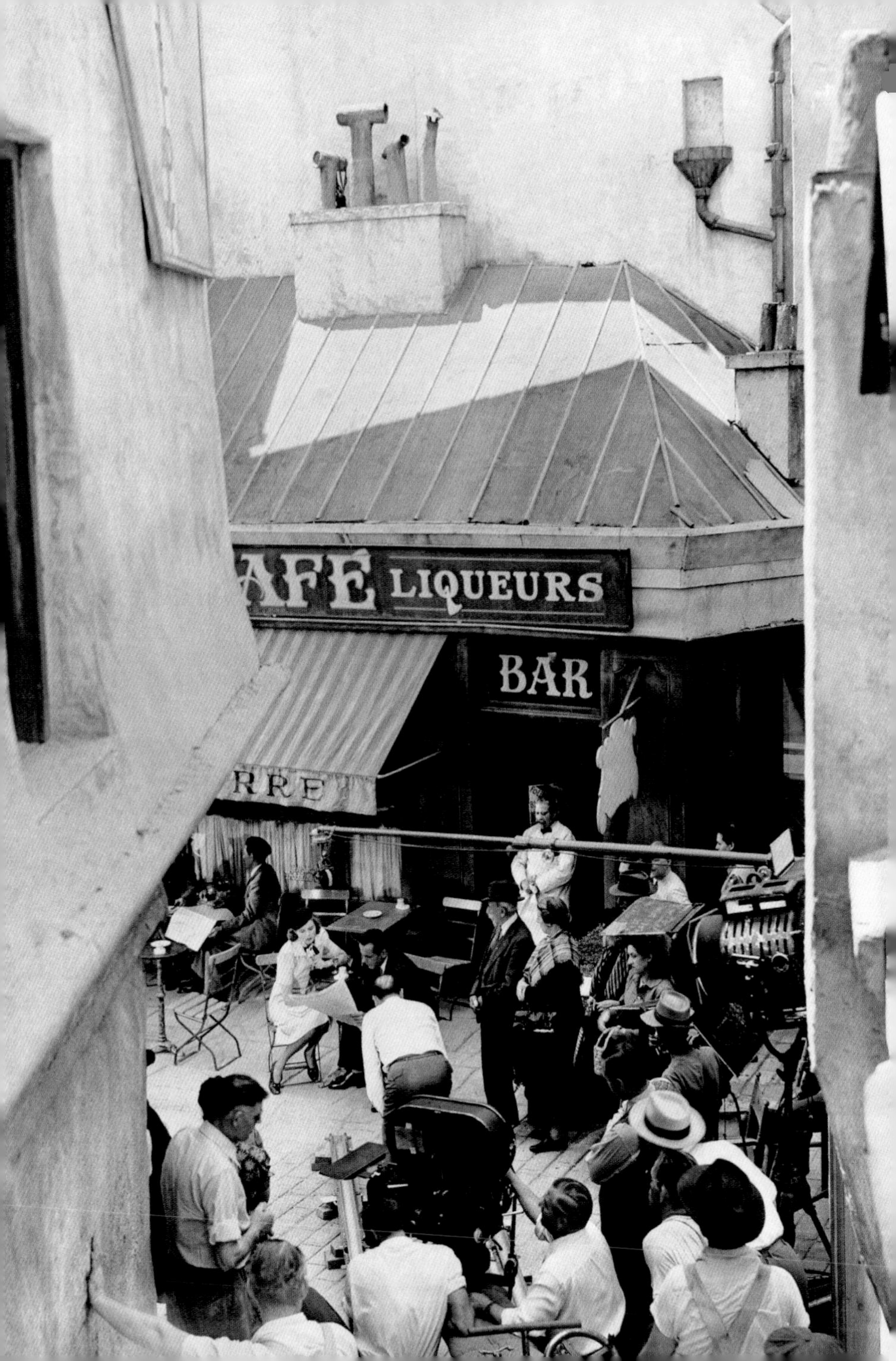
AFÉ LIQUEURS
BAR
RRE

STILL FROM 'CASABLANCA' (1942)
"If she can stand it, I can. Play it." / „Wenn sie es aushält, halte auch ich es aus. Spiel's." / « Si elle peut le supporter, moi aussi. Joue ! »

"Of all the gin joints, in all the towns, in all the world, she had to walk into mine."
Rick Blaine, 'Casablanca' (1942)

„Von allen Kaschemmen in allen Städten der ganzen Welt kommt sie ausgerechnet in meine."
Rick Blaine, *Casablanca* (1942)

« De tous les bars, de toutes les villes dans le monde, il fallait qu'elle entre dans le mien ! »
Rick Blaine, *Casablanca* (1942)

SONGSHEET FOR 'AS TIME GOES BY' (1942)

STILL FROM 'CASABLANCA' (1942)
The love triangle plus one. Ingrid, her husband Paul
Henreid, her lover Bogart, and the slippery Captain
Claude Rains defy the Nazis. / Das Dreiecksverhältnis
plus eins. Ilsa (Bergman), ihr Ehemann Victor (Paul
Henreid), ihr Liebhaber Rick (Bogart) und der gerissene
Capitaine Renault (Claude Rains) schlagen den Nazis
ein Schnippchen. / Ilsa (Ingrid Bergman), son mari (Paul
Henreid), son amant (Bogart) et le capitaine Renault
(Claude Rains) défient les nazis.

STILL FROM 'CASABLANCA' (1942)
A mess of a production that no one thought would live
beyond the year of release, 'Casablanca' has become
immortal. / Die Produktion verlief so chaotisch, dass
kaum jemand glaubte, man würde sich im nächsten Jahr
noch an den Film erinnern – doch *Casablanca* wurde
unsterblich. / Tourné en catastrophe, ce film sur lequel
personne n'aurait parié un sou deviendra un immortel
chef-d'œuvre.

*"Anytime that Ingrid Bergman looks at a man, he
has sex appeal."*
Humphrey Bogart

*„Jedesmal, wenn Ingrid Bergman einen Mann
anschaut, dann hat er Sex-Appeal."*
Humphrey Bogart

*« Chaque fois qu'Ingrid Bergman regarde un
homme, il a du sex-appeal. »*
Humphrey Bogart

**STILL FROM 'ACTION IN THE NORTH
ATLANTIC' (1943)**
Merchant marine lieutenant Bogart confers with captain
Raymond Massey to battle the Nazis. / Als Leutnant
der Handelsmarine berät Bogart mit dem Kapitän
(Raymond Massey), wie man die Nazis schlagen
könnte. / Lieutenant dans la marine marchande, Bogart
discute avec le capitaine (Raymond Massey) pour
combattre les nazis.

**STILL FROM 'ACTION IN THE NORTH
ATLANTIC' (1943)**
Bogart on lookout. / Bogart am Ausguck. / Bogart en
vigie.

STILL FROM 'SAHARA' (1943)
Classic propaganda film with tank commander Bogart defeating the Germans in the North African desert. / Ein klassischer Propagandafilm mit Bogart als Panzerkommandant, der in der Wüste von Nordafrika erfolgreich deutsche Truppen bekämpft. / Film de propagande où le commandant d'un tank (Bogart) défait les Allemands dans le désert nord-africain.

STILL FROM 'PASSAGE TO MARSEILLE' (1944)
To capitalize on the success of 'Casablanca,' Warners reunited director and cast, with only limited success. / Um aus dem Erfolg von *Casablanca* Kapital zu schlagen, bringt Warner Bros. den Regisseur und die Hauptdarsteller des Films noch einmal zusammen, allerdings mit mäßigem Erfolg. / La Warner réunit à nouveau les acteurs et le réalisateur de *Casablanca*, sans pour autant obtenir le même succès.

STILL FROM 'TO HAVE AND HAVE NOT' (1944)
Bogart finds his equal in the sassy nightclub performer
and anti-fascist Lauren Bacall. / Bogart findet eine
Gleichgesinnte in der dreisten Nachtclubsängerin und
Widerstandskämpferin „Slim" (Lauren Bacall). / Harry
(Bogart) trouve son double dans une belle insolente qui
chante dans les bars (Lauren Bacall).

PAGES 112/113
STILL FROM 'PASSAGE TO MARSEILLE' (1944)
As Jean Matrac, Bogart escapes Devil's Island to fight
the French fascists, literally and figuratively. / Als Jean
Matrac kann Bogart von der Teufelsinsel fliehen, um
gegen französische Faschisten zu kämpfen - sowohl im
wörtlichen als auch im übertragenen Sinn. / Jean
Matrac (Bogart) s'échappe de l'île du Diable pour
combattre le régime de Vichy.

**PORTRAIT FOR 'TO HAVE AND HAVE NOT'
(1944)**
The film initiated a real-life relationship between Bogart
and Bacall that continued until his death. / Mit dem Film
begann auch die private Beziehung zwischen Bogart
und Bacall, die bis zu seinem Tod andauerte. / Entre
Bogart et Bacall, ce tournage marque le début d'un
amour qui durera jusqu'à sa mort.

ON THE SET OF 'CONFLICT' (1945)
Bogart often played chess on the set and was quite proficient, revealing his more intellectual side. / Dass Bogart während der Dreharbeiten oft Schach spielte und darin recht gut war, zeigte seine intellektuellere Seite. / Grand adepte des échecs sur les plateaux de tournage, Bogart révèle ainsi son côté cérébral.

STILL FROM 'CONFLICT' (1945)
In this classic noir film Bogart sinks deeper into the world of murder, madness, and deception. / In diesem Klassiker des *Film noir* versinkt Bogart als Richard Mason immer tiefer in einem Morast aus Mord, Wahnsinn und Betrug. / Un classique du genre où Bogart s'enfonce dans un monde de violence, de mensonge et de folie.

STILL FROM 'THE BIG SLEEP' (1946)
After nailing noir detective Sam Spade for future
generations, Bogart does the same for Raymond
Chandler's Philip Marlowe. / Nachdem er die Figur des
Film-noir-Privatdetektivs Sam Spade für alle Zeiten
festgelegt hatte, tat Bogart hier das Gleiche für
Raymond Chandlers Philip Marlowe. / Après avoir
immortalisé le personnage de Sam Spade, Bogart en fait
de même pour le détective Philip Marlowe de Raymond
Chandler.

STILL FROM 'THE BIG SLEEP' (1946)

STILL FROM 'THE BIG SLEEP' (1946)
The "bad sister" Carmen Sternwood (Martha Vickers),
drug addict and nymphomaniac, brings out the
reluctant "knight errant" in Marlowe. / Vivians
„böse Schwester" Carmen (Martha Vickers), eine
drogenabhängige Nymphomanin, bringt den „fahrenden
Ritter wider Willen" in Marlowe zum Vorschein. /
Carmen Sternwood (Martha Vickers), nymphomane
droguée, révèle le « chevalier errant » qui sommeille en
Marlowe.

STILL FROM 'THE BIG SLEEP' (1946)
Lauren Bacall, as the sensual and level-headed Vivian
Sternwood, helps Marlowe out of another scrape. /
In der Rolle der sinnlichen und besonnenen Vivian
Sternwood hilft Lauren Bacall Marlowe wieder einmal
aus der Patsche. / Pleine de sensualité et de sang-froid,
Vivian Sternwood (Lauren Bacall) sort Marlowe d'un
mauvais pas.

PORTRAIT
In 1946 Bogart became the highest-paid actor in
the world, allowing him to afford the luxuries of life, like
golf ... / Im Jahre 1946 wurde Bogart zum bestbezahlten
Schauspieler der Welt, so dass er sich luxuriöse Hobbys
leisten konnte – wie zum Beispiel das Golfen ... /
En 1946, Bogart devient l'acteur le mieux payé au
monde. À lui les joies du golf ...

PORTRAIT
... and sailing. Bogart would soon purchase his beloved
yacht *Santana*. / ... und das Segeln. Wenig später kaufte
sich Bogart seine geliebte Jacht *Santana*. / ... et de la
plaisance, à bord notamment de son yacht, le Santana.

PAGES 124/125
STILL FROM 'DEAD RECKONING' (1947)
Bogart refines the character of the alienated veteran
who finds his doom in *femme fatale* Lizabeth Scott. /
Bogart verfeinert die Figur des entfremdeten
Veteranen, den eine *Femme fatale* (Lizabeth Scott) ins
Verderben stürzt. / Bogart peaufine son personnage
d'ancien combattant désabusé qui croise son destin
sous les traits d'une femme fatale (Lizabeth Scott).

COMMITTEE FOR THE FIRST AMENDMENT (1947)
Bogart and Bacall lead a group of actors to protest the Red 'witch hunts' perpetrated by the HUAC hearings. / Bogart und Bacall führen eine Gruppe von Schauspielern an, die gegen die „Hexenjagd" auf Kommunisten durch die Anhörungen des HUAC protestieren. / Bogart et Bacall à la tête d'un groupe d'acteurs venus protester contre la « chasse aux sorcières » au sein de l'industrie cinématographique.

PAGES 128/129
STILL FROM 'DARK PASSAGE' (1947)
Bogart is an escaped convict who has his face altered and tries to clear his name. / Bogart spielt einen Ausbrecher, der sein Gesicht operativ verändern lässt, um anschließend Beweise für seine Unschuld zu sammeln. / Bogart en prisonnier évadé qui s'est fait refaire le visage pour tenter de prouver son innocence.

PORTRAIT FOR 'THE TWO MRS. CARROLLS' (1947)
Bogart does not excel at playing a long-suffering artist in this gothic mystery with Barbara Stanwyck. / Der leidende Künstler, den Bogart in diesem Gruselfilm mit Barbara Stanwyck spielt, scheint ihm nicht zu liegen. / Bogart n'est guère à son aise dans ce mystère gothique où il incarne un artiste tourmenté aux côtés de Barbara Stanwyck.

ON THE SET OF 'DARK PASSAGE' (1947)
The fight with Young is neatly choreographed by
director Delmer Daves. / Der Kampf mit Young
wurde von Regisseur Delmer Daves sorgfältig
choreographiert. / Le corps à corps avec Young est
parfaitement chorégraphié par le réalisateur Delmer
Daves.

STILL FROM 'DARK PASSAGE' (1947)
Bogart confronts criminal Clifton Young to unravel the
complex mystery concocted by noir novelist David
Goodis. / Bogart stellt den Verbrecher Baker (Clifton
Young) zur Rede, um das komplexe Geheimnis zu lüften,
das sich der Krimi-Autor David Goodis ausgedacht hat. /
Bogart affronte le criminel (Clifton Young) pour
élucider l'épais mystère concocté par le romancier
David Goodis.

ON THE SET OF 'THE TREASURE OF THE SIERRA MADRE' (1948)
The cast and crew try to cool off in the hot Mexican sun. / Stab und Schauspieler suchen Abkühlung in der Hitze Mexikos. / Acteurs et techniciens tentent de se rafraîchir sous le soleil torride du Mexique.

ON THE SET OF 'THE TREASURE OF THE SIERRA MADRE' (1948)
Director John Huston (foreground) confers with Bogart, who plays the wily and greedy Fred C. Dobbs. / Regisseur John Huston (vorn) berät sich mit Bogart, der den verschlagenen und raffgierigen Fred C. Dobbs spielt. / Le réalisateur John Huston (au premier plan) discute avec Bogart, qui campe un aventurier rusé et rapace.

"Himself, he never took too seriously – his work, most seriously. He regarded the somewhat gaudy figure of Bogart, the star, with amused cynicism; Bogart, the actor, he held in deep respect."
John Huston, producer/director

„*Er nahm sich selbst nie besonders ernst, seine Arbeit dafür umso mehr. Er betrachtete die etwas schillernde Figur des Stars Bogart amüsiert zynisch, aber vor dem Schauspieler Bogart zeigte er große Ehrfurcht.*"
John Huston, Produzent/Regisseur

« *Lui-même, il ne se prenait jamais très au sérieux, mais son travail, c'était une autre affaire. Il considérait le personnage quelque peu tapageur de Bogart la star avec un cynisme amusé, mais pour Bogart l'acteur, il avait le plus grand respect.* »
John Huston, producteur/réalisateur

STILL FROM 'THE TREASURE OF THE SIERRA MADRE' (1948)
Walter Huston, the director's father, as the cantankerous prospector and Dobbs as his partner in treasure hunting. / Walter Huston, der Vater des Regisseurs, geht in der Rolle des mürrischen Goldsuchers Howard mit seinem Partner Dobbs auf Schatzsuche. / Walter Huston, le père du réalisateur, en chercheur d'or irascible auquel Dobbs (Bogart) va s'associer.

ON THE SET OF 'KEY LARGO' (1948)
Bogart took his craft seriously and was one of the
hardest working actors in Hollywood. / Bogart nahm
sein Handwerk ernst und gehörte zu den am härtesten
arbeitenden Schauspielern in Hollywood. / Bogart, qui
prend son métier très au sérieux, est l'un des
comédiens les plus bosseurs de Hollywood.

ON THE SET OF 'KEY LARGO' (1948)

138

ON THE SET OF 'KEY LARGO' (1948)
Husband and wife share intimacy, as well as cigarettes, on the set. / Das Ehepaar gönnt sich während der Dreharbeiten eine Zigarettenpause zu zweit. / Instant d'intimité entre mari et femme, le temps d'une cigarette sur le plateau de tournage.

ON THE SET OF 'KEY LARGO' (1948)
As well as being hard-drinking buddies, Huston and Bogart were also consummate professionals. / Huston und Bogart waren nicht nur Trinkkumpane, sondern auch Vollprofis. / Leurs beuveries communes n'empêchent pas Huston et Bogart d'être des professionnels accomplis.

STILL FROM 'KNOCK ON ANY DOOR' (1949)
Bogart formed his own production company, Santana, and starred in its first film with John Derek. / Nach der Gründung seiner eigenen Produktionsfirma Santana spielte Bogart in seinem ersten Film neben John Derek auch eine der Hauptrollen. / Bogart joue avec John Derek dans le premier film de sa propre maison de production.

"I'm not good looking. I used to be, but not anymore. Not like Robert Taylor. What I have got is I have character in my face. When I go to work in a picture I say, 'Don't take the lines out of my face. Leave them there.'"
Humphrey Bogart

„Ich sehe nicht gut aus. Früher mal, aber jetzt nicht mehr. Nicht wie Robert Taylor. Aber ich habe ein Charaktergesicht. Wenn ich einen Film drehe, dann sage ich: ‚Nehmt die Falten nicht aus meinem Gesicht raus. Lasst sie da.'"
Humphrey Bogart

STILL FROM 'TOKYO JOE' (1949)
This mediocre reworking of 'Casablanca' was the kind
of film Warners forced him to do. / Dieser mittelmäßige
Aufguss von *Casablanca* war typisch für die Filme, zu
denen Warner Bros. Bogart zwang. / Ce médiocre
remake de *Casablanca* est le type de films que la
Warner le contraint à tourner.

« Je ne suis pas beau. Je l'ai été, mais plus
maintenant. Pas comme *Robert Taylor*. Ce que j'ai,
c'est un visage qui a du caractère. Quand je joue
dans un film, je dis "N'effacez pas les rides de mon
visage. Laissez-les." »
Humphrey Bogart

STILL FROM 'CHAIN LIGHTNING' (1950)
This was little better than 'Tokyo Joe.' / Auch dieser
Film war kaum besser als *Tokio-Joe.* / Un autre film qui
ne vaut guère mieux que *Tokyo Joe.*

PORTRAIT (1949)
The ecstatic parents with their brand-new baby
Stephen. / Die stolzen Eltern sind von ihrem neuen
Spross Stephen ganz hingerissen. / Des parents en
adoration devant leur nouveau-né, Stephen.

DAMAGED MAN

ANGESCHLAGEN

L'HOMME BLESSÉ

STILL FROM 'IN A LONELY PLACE' (1950)
Bogart becomes angered at what he perceives as his
lover Gloria Grahame's act of disloyalty. / Bogart ist
verärgert über die vermeintliche Untreue seiner
Geliebten (Gloria Grahame). / Dixon (Bogart), furieux
de ce qu'il perçoit comme un manque de loyauté de la
part de sa maîtresse (Gloria Grahame).

PAGE 144
PORTRAIT FOR 'IN A LONELY PLACE' (1950)
Bogart as Dixon Steele, a disturbed and disturbing
character. / Bogart als Dixon Steele, eine ebenso
verstörte wie verstörende Figur. / Bogart alias Dixon
Steele, personnage dérangé et dérangeant.

STILL FROM 'IN A LONELY PLACE' (1950)
The film is both Bogart and director Nicholas Ray's
meditation on alcoholism and male violence,
dysfunctions both men were familiar with. / Sowohl
Bogart als auch Regisseur Nicholas Ray sinnierten
in diesem Film über Alkoholismus und männliche Gewalt – Charakterstörungen, die beiden vertraut waren. /
Ce film est une réflexion de Bogart et du réalisateur
Nicholas Ray sur l'alcoolisme et la violence masculine,
dysfonctionnements dont les deux hommes sont
familiers.

"Whatever it is, be against it."
Humphrey Bogart

„Was auch immer es sein mag, sei dagegen."
Humphrey Bogart

« De quoi qu'il s'agisse, soyez contre. »
Humphrey Bogart

STILL FROM 'IN A LONELY PLACE' (1950)
Bogart lets both his age and his alienation shine through
in this brutally honest portrait of a man consumed by his
demons. / In diesem brutal aufrichtigen Porträt eines
Mannes, der von seinen Dämonen verzehrt wird, lässt
Bogart sowohl sein Alter als auch seine eigene
Entfremdung durchblitzen. / Bogart laisse son âge et
son aliénation transparaître dans ce portrait honnête
et brutal d'un homme rongé par ses démons.

STILL FROM 'THE ENFORCER' (1951)
Bogart's last performance for Warners; a film he
considered "out of date" when it was made. / Bogart
empfand seinen letzten Film für Warner Bros. schon
zum Zeitpunkt der Produktion als „überholt". / Le
dernier rôle de Bogart pour la Warner, un film qu'il
considère «démodé» dès sa sortie.

"Gary Cooper is not a great actor, but Spencer
Tracy is. I'm not a great actor, but when we,
Coop and I, come on screen people focus attention
on us."
Humphrey Bogart

„Gary Cooper ist kein großer Schauspieler, im
Unterschied zu Spencer Tracy. Ich selbst bin kein
großer Schauspieler, aber wenn wir – Coop und
ich – auf die Leinwand kommen, dann richtet sich
die Aufmerksamkeit der Zuschauer auf uns."
Humphrey Bogart

«Gary Cooper n'est pas un grand acteur,
contrairement à Spencer Tracy. Je ne suis pas un
grand acteur non plus, mais Coop et moi, quand
nous apparaissons à l'écran, l'attention se focalise
sur nous.»
Humphrey Bogart

STILL FROM 'SIROCCO' (1951)
'Casablanca' again, as another amoral man is caught in the middle of a battle for freedom. / Schon wieder *Casablanca* - und wieder spielt Bogart einen amoralischen Menschen, der in einen Freiheitskampf verstrickt wird. / Encore une histoire inspirée de *Casablanca*, celle d'un homme amoral pris dans un combat pour la liberté.

STILL FROM 'THE AFRICAN QUEEN' (1951)
John Huston comes to the rescue again and lifts Bogart
out of mediocrity to help him win an Academy Award. /
Wieder kommt ihm John Huston zu Hilfe und rettet
Bogart aus dem Mittelmaß mit einer Rolle, für die er mit
einem Academy Award („Oscar") ausgezeichnet wird. /
John Huston arrive à la rescousse pour sortir Bogart de
la médiocrité et l'aider à remporter un Oscar.

*"Well I ain't sorry for you no more, you crazy,
psalm-singing, skinny old maid."*
Charlie Allnut to Rose, 'The African Queen' (1951)

*„Aber jetzt Sie tun mir nicht mehr leid, Sie
verrückte, psalmensingende, dürre alte Jungfer."*
Charlie Allnut zu Rose, *African Queen* (1951)

*« Eh bien, je n'ai plus pitié de vous, espèce de
vieille fille maigrichonne, bigote et cinglée. »*
Charlie Allnut à Rose, *L'Odyssée de l'African Queen* (1951)

STILL FROM 'THE AFRICAN QUEEN' (1951)
Bogart draws on his now-legendary orneriness to sculpt the character of Charlie Allnut. / Bogart lässt seine schon legendäre schlechte Laune spielen, um der Figur des Charlie Allnut Charakter zu verleihen. / Bogart puise dans son sale caractère désormais légendaire pour forger le personnage de Charlie Allnut.

PAGES 154/155
STILL FROM 'THE AFRICAN QUEEN' (1951)
Katharine Hepburn suffered as much as Bogart during the difficult African shoot. This scene was shot in England. / Während der schwierigen Dreharbeiten in Afrika litt Katharine Hepburn ebenso wie Bogart. Diese Szene entstand allerdings in England. / Il n'y a pas qu'en Afrique que Katharine Hepburn et Bogart souffrent des conditions de tournage, puisque cette scène est filmée en Angleterre.

STILL FROM 'THE AFRICAN QUEEN' (1951)
The film evidenced the obvious respect and chemistry
that existed between Hepburn and Bogart. / Der Film
zeigte den offensichtlichen gegenseitigen Respekt und
die Chemie zwischen Hepburn und Bogart. / Ce film
met en évidence le respect et la connivence qui
unissent Hepburn et Bogart.

"Bogart, in what is very likely the best performance
of his long career, plays a man who is crude only
on the surface; there is a goodness underneath his
unshaven appearance."
Bosley Crowther, critic, on 'The African Queen' (1951)

„In der wahrscheinlich besten schauspielerischen
Leistung seiner langen Karriere spielt Bogart einen
Mann, in dessen harter Schale ein weicher Kern
steckt: Unter seinem unrasierten Äußeren schlägt
ein gutes Herz."
Kritiker Bosley Crowther über *African Queen* (1951)

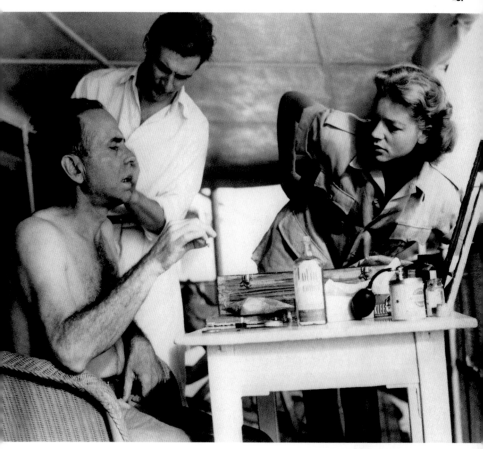

ON THE SET OF 'THE AFRICAN QUEEN' (1951)
Bacall was a constant source of support for Bogart
during the shoot. / Während der Dreharbeiten stand
Bacall ihrem Ehemann stets zur Seite. / Bacall offre un
soutien constant à son mari durant le tournage.

« Bogart, dans ce qui est sûrement la meilleure
interprétation de sa longue carrière, joue un
homme qui n'est grossier qu'en surface ; il y a
de la bonté sous son air mal rasé. »
Le critique Bosley Crowther au sujet de L'Odyssée de
l'African Queen (1951)

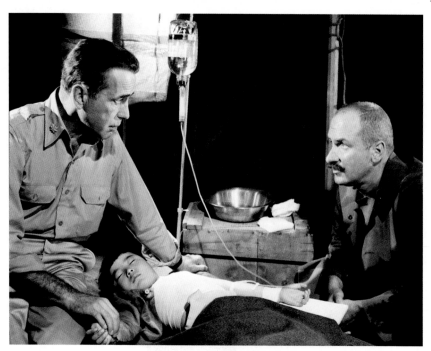

STILL FROM 'BATTLE CIRCUS' (1953)
Bogart as an Army doctor in the Korean war, with
Keenan Wynn as his sergeant. / Bogart spielt einen
Feldarzt im Koreakrieg, Keenan Wynn seinen
Feldwebel. / Bogart en médecin militaire pendant la
guerre de Corée, avec Keenan Wynn pour sergent.

STILL FROM 'DEADLINE U.S.A.' (1952)
Bogart as a dedicated reporter, in this hard-hitting
and critically well-received story of investigative
journalism. / Bogart spielt in dieser schonungslosen und
von der Kritik gelobten Geschichte über investigativen
Journalismus einen Reporter, der ganz in seiner Arbeit
aufgeht. / Bogart en reporter consciencieux, dans un
film percutant sur le journalisme d'investigation.

STILL FROM 'BEAT THE DEVIL' (1953)
A disparate cast, including Bogart and Gina Lollobrigida, populates this tongue-in-cheek tale concocted by John Huston and Truman Capote. / Eine ungleiche Schauspielerriege, zu der auch Bogart und Gina Lollobrigida zählten, erweckte diese ironische Geschichte, die sich John Huston und Truman Capote ausgedacht hatten, zum Leben. / Bogart et Gina Lollobrigida dans une distribution disparate, pour cette fable ironique concoctée par John Huston et Truman Capote.

"I defend my right to cut a caper if I feel like it, a man has the right to get rotten drunk and raise some trouble. The trouble with these young male stars today is that they have no color, no imagination."
Humphrey Bogart

„Ich bestehe auf meinem Recht, hin und wieder Dummheiten zu machen, wenn mir danach ist. Ein Mann hat das Recht, sich sinnlos zu besaufen und die Sau rauszulassen. Das Problem bei den männlichen Jungstars von heute ist, dass sie so farblos und so einfallslos sind."
Humphrey Bogart

STILL FROM 'BEAT THE DEVIL' (1953)
Bogart with his omnipresent drink and a black eye for
good measure. / Bogart mit seinem allgegenwärtigen
Drink und obendrein einem blauen Auge. / Bogart avec
son éternel verre à la main et un œil au beurre noir pour
faire bonne mesure.

PAGES 162/163
ON THE SET OF 'BEAT THE DEVIL' (1953)
Cast and crew take a break: Bogart is in black overcoat;
Huston sits middle; Peter Lorre reclines. / Stab und
Schauspieler legen eine Pause ein: Bogart im schwarzen
Mantel, Huston sitzend in der Mitte, Peter Lorre
zurückgelehnt. / L'heure de la pause : Bogart en
manteau noir, Huston assis au milieu, Peter Lorre
étendu.

*« Je défends mon droit à faire le fou si j'en ai envie,
tout le monde a le droit de boire comme un trou
et de semer la pagaille. Le problème des jeunes
vedettes masculines, aujourd'hui, c'est qu'elles
n'ont ni couleur, ni imagination. »*
Humphrey Bogart

STILL FROM 'THE CAINE MUTINY' (1954)
Queeg rules with an iron hand on his ship. / Queeg herrscht mit eiserner Hand über sein Schiff. / Queeg règne d'une poigne de fer sur son équipage.

"Ahh, but the strawberries, that's ... that's where I had them. They laughed at me and made jokes bu I proved beyond the shadow of a doubt and with .. geometric logic ..."
Lt. Commander Queeg, 'The Caine Mutiny' (1954)

„Ahh, aber die Erdbeeren, die ... die hatte ich doch hier. Sie lachten mich aus und machten Witze, aber ich konnte zweifelsfrei beweisen und mit ... geometrischer Logik ..."
Lieutenant Commander Queeg, *Die Caine war ihr Schicksal* (1954)

« Ah, mais les fraises, c'est ... c'est là que je les ai eus. Ils ont ri et se sont moqués de moi, mais j'ai prouvé sans l'ombre d'un doute et avec ... une logique géométrique ... »
Commandant Queeg, *Ouragan sur le Caine* (1954)

STILL FROM 'THE CAINE MUTINY' (1954)
A deeply damaged man: Lt. Cmdr. Philip Francis Queeg. / Ein schwer angeschlagener Mensch: Lieutenant Commander Philip Francis Queeg. / Un homme profondément perturbé : le commandant Philip Francis Queeg

STILL FROM 'SABRINA' (1954)
Bogart is an uptight business man who is disgusted with
his playboy younger brother William Holden. / Bogart
spielt einen verklemmten Geschäftsmann, der vom
Lebenswandel seines jüngeren Bruders, des Playboys
David (William Holden), angewidert ist. / Bogart en
homme d'affaires rigide, dégoûté par la vie de play-boy
de son frère cadet (William Holden).

STILL FROM 'SABRINA' (1954)
Drawing on his May-December relationship with
wife Bacall, Bogart romances the vivacious Audrey
Hepburn. / Für seine Romanze mit der lebhaften
Sabrina (Audrey Hepburn) kann Bogart aus seinen
eigenen Erfahrungen mit seiner wesentlich jüngeren
Frau Lauren Bacall schöpfen. / S'inspirant de sa
différence d'âge avec sa propre femme, Bogart conte
fleurette à la pétillante Audrey Hepburn.

**STILL FROM 'THE BAREFOOT CONTESSA'
(1954)**
Two rebels: Ava Gardner and Bogart. / Zwei Rebellen:
Ava Gardner und Bogart. / Deux rebelles : Ava Gardner
et Bogart.

STILL FROM 'SABRINA' (1954)
Bogart is tender. / Bogart ganz zärtlich. / Bogart tendre.

STILL FROM 'WE'RE NO ANGELS' (1955)
Bogart allows his humorous side to shine in this comic period tale of escaped convicts. / Bogart zeigte in dieser Ausbrecherkomödie einmal seine witzige Seite. / Bogart laisse percer son humour dans cette histoire de prisonniers évadés.

STILL FROM 'WE'RE NO ANGELS' (1955)
The three devilish angels (Aldo Ray, Bogart, and Peter Ustinov) spy on the fetching Joan Bennett. / Die drei teuflischen Engel (Aldo Ray, Bogart und Peter Ustinov) beobachten heimlich die attraktive Joan Bennett. / Trois anges démoniaques (Aldo Ray, Bogart et Peter Ustinov) épient la ravissante Joan Bennett.

"I expected a lot more from me. And I'm never going to get it."
Humphrey Bogart

„Ich hatte viel mehr von mir erwartet. Und ich werde es nie erreichen."
Humphrey Bogart

« J'en attendais beaucoup plus de moi. Et je ne l'obtiendrai jamais. »
Humphrey Bogart

STILL FROM 'THE LEFT HAND OF GOD' (1955)
Dissatisfied with his performance in this film, Bogart yearned for tougher, grittier roles. / Bogart war mit seiner eigenen Leistung in diesem Film unzufrieden und sehnte sich nach härteren, bodenständigeren Rollen. / Mécontent de son interprétation dans ce film, Bogart aspire à des rôles plus durs et plus réalistes.

STILL FROM 'THE DESPERATE HOURS' (1955)
Bogart leads three psychopathic escaped convicts who
kidnap a middle-class family. / Bogart spielt den
Anführer der drei ausgebrochenen Psychopathen, die
eine bürgerliche Familie als Geiseln nehmen. / Bogart,
l'un des trois psychopathes en cavale qui prennent une
famille en otage.

"When the heavy, full of crime and bitterness,
grabs his wounds and talks about death, the
audience is his and his alone."
Humphrey Bogart

„Wenn sich der Bösewicht, voller Kriminalität und
Verbitterung, an seine Wunden fasst und über den
Tod redet, dann gehört das Publikum ganz ihm und
ihm alleine."
Humphrey Bogart

« Quand le truand, plein de crimes et d'amertume,
porte la main à ses plaies et parle de la mort, le
public lui est totalement acquis. »
Humphrey Bogart

STILL FROM 'THE DESPERATE HOURS' (1955)
Director William Wyler kept up the tension. /
Regisseur William Wyler hielt die Spannung aufrecht. /
Le réalisateur William Wyler fait monter la tension.

STILL FROM 'THE HARDER THEY FALL' (1956)
Bogart's swan song was a brilliant dissection of a
conflicted, morally dubious journalist. / Bogarts
Schwanengesang war die glänzende Analyse eines
hin- und hergerissenen Journalisten von zweifelhafter
Moral. / Pour son chant du cygne, Bogart dissèque
admirablement l'âme d'un journaliste à la morale
douteuse.

*"You're crazy if you think you'll make a hero out of
him, the son of a bitch lisps."*
**Assistant director Paul Schwagler to director Tay Garnett
in 1937**

*„Du spinnst, wenn du glaubst, du kannst aus dem
einen Helden machen – der Hurensohn lispelt
doch."*
**Regieassistent Paul Schwagler zu Regisseur Tay Garnett
im Jahre 1937**

*« Vous êtes fou de penser que vous en ferez un
héros, le pauvre bougre a un cheveu sur la
langue. »*
**L'assistant-réalisateur Paul Schwagler au réalisateur Tay
Garnett, en 1937**

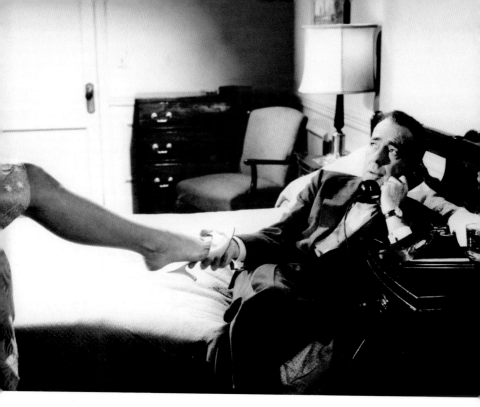

STILL FROM 'THE HARDER THEY FALL' (1956)
Bogart faces temptation of all kinds in the film. /
Bogart musste in diesem Film Versuchungen
unterschiedlichster Art widerstehen. / Bogart
en proie à toutes sortes de tentations.

PAGE 178
PORTRAIT (1945)
Lauren Bacall and Humphrey Bogart. / Lauren Bacall
und Humphrey Bogart. / Lauren Bacall et Humphrey
Bogart.

3

CHRONOLOGY

CHRONOLOGIE

CHRONOLOGIE

1899 Humphrey DeForest Bogart born on 25 December in New York City, to Maud Humphrey, a prominent artist, and Belmont, a doctor.

1918 Bogart expelled from Phillips Academy because of low grades.

1920 While working as an office boy for World Films given the chance to direct *Life* but is fired.

1922 First Broadway role in the play *Drifting*.

1926 Marries theatrical star Helen Menken.

1928 Marries actress Mary Philips.

1930 Dissatisfied with his stage career, Bogart signs with Fox and moves to Los Angeles but gets a series of undistinguished roles.

1932 Columbia signs Bogart to a contract. Again the roles are minor, so he divides his time between stage and screen.

1935 Plays gangster Duke Mantee in Robert E. Sherwood's play *The Petrified Forest*. Leslie Howard insists that Bogart is also hired for the film. Warner Bros. signs Bogart to a contract.

1937 Appears in William Wyler's *Dead End* as the gangster Baby Face Martin. He divorces Mary.

1938 Meets writer John Huston during the production of *The Amazing Dr. Clitterhouse* and they become lifelong friends and drinking buddies. Bogart marries Mayo Methot in August.

1940 Bogart testifies before the Special Committee on Un-American Activities that he was never a member of the Communist Party.

1941 *High Sierra* is a hit, financially and critically. It opens the way to more important, multidimensional parts. Bogart stars in John Huston's adaptation of Dashiell Hammett's *The Maltese Falcon*. It is also a success.

1942 *Casablanca* is a box-office hit, solidifying the iconic status of Humphrey Bogart in the role of the noir anti-hero Rick Blaine.

1944 Bogart meets teenage model Lauren Bacall while making *To Have and Have Not*. They begin an affair and collaborate on noir classics like *The Big Sleep*, *Dark Passage*, and *Key Largo*.

1945 Divorces Mayo and marries Bacall.

1946 A new contract with Warner Bros. gives him veto power over his projects for them and makes him among the highest-paid stars in Hollywood.

1947 Bogart, Bacall and other actors go to Washington to protest the 'witch hunts' of the House Un-American Activities Committee.

1948 Bogart forms his own production company, Santana. He stars in John Huston's classic *The Treasure of the Sierra Madre*.

1949 Bogart's son Stephen is born.

1950 Bogart produces and stars in one of the mainstays of film noir: *In a Lonely Place*, directed by Nicholas Ray.

1952 Wins an Academy Award for *The African Queen*. His daughter Leslie Howard (in honor of the actor) is born.

1954 Plays the mentally unstable Queeg in *The Caine Mutiny* and receives critical raves.

1956 Develops cancer of the esophagus.

1957 Humphrey DeForest Bogart dies on 14 January.

CHRONOLOGIE

1899 Humphrey DeForest Bogart wird in New York am Weihnachtstag als Sohn der bekannten Zeichnerin Maud Humphrey und des Arztes Dr. Belmont Bogart geboren.

1918 Wegen schlechter Schulnoten muss Bogart die Phillips Academy verlassen.

1920 Während er für World Films als Laufbursche arbeitet, erhält er die Chance, bei dem Film *Life* Regie zu führen, wird jedoch gefeuert.

1922 Er erhält seine erste Rolle am Broadway in dem Theaterstück *Drifting*.

1926 Er heiratet den Bühnenstar Helen Menken.

1928 Er heiratet die Schauspielerin Mary Philips.

1930 Mit seiner Theaterkarriere unzufrieden, unterschreibt Bogart einen Filmvertrag bei Fox und zieht nach Los Angeles, erhält dort aber nur banale Nebenrollen.

1932 Columbia nimmt Bogart unter Vertrag. Auch hier sind die Rollen klein, so dass ihm neben dem Film noch ausreichend Zeit für die Bühne bleibt.

1935 Er spielt den Gangster Duke Mantee in dem Drama *Der versteinerte Wald* von Robert E. Sherwood. Leslie Howard besteht darauf, dass Bogart die Rolle auch in der Verfilmung erhält. Warner Bros. nimmt Bogart unter Vertrag.

1937 Er tritt in William Wylers *Sackgasse* als Gangster Baby Face Martin auf. Im gleichen Jahr lässt er sich von Mary scheiden.

1938 Er trifft den Autor John Huston während der Dreharbeiten zu *Das Doppelleben des Dr. Clitterhouse*, und die beiden werden Freunde und Trinkkumpane fürs Leben. Bogart heiratet im August Mayo Methot.

1940 Bogart sagt vor dem Sonderausschuss des Repräsentantenhauses zur Untersuchung unamerikanischer Umtriebe (HUAC) aus, dass er zu keinem Zeitpunkt Mitglied der Kommunistischen Partei war.

PORTRAIT
Humphrey Bogart plays cards with Peter Lorre. /
Humphrey Bogart beim Kartenspiel mit Peter Lorre. /
Partie de cartes avec Peter Lorre.

1941 *Entscheidung in der Sierra* wird bei den Kritikern und an der Kasse zum Erfolg und ebnet Bogart den Weg für wichtigere und vielschichtigere Rollen. Bogart erhält die Hauptrolle in John Hustons Verfilmung des Kriminalromans *Der Malteser Falke* von Dashiell Hammett. Auch dieser Film ist erfolgreich

1942 *Casablanca* mit Humphrey Bogart in der Rolle des Film-noir-Antihelden Rick Blaine wird zum Kassenschlager und festigt seinen Status als Ikone.

1944 Bogart trifft bei den Dreharbeiten zu *Haben und Nichthaben* das zwanzigjährige Fotomodell Lauren Bacall. Aus ihrer Affäre wird später eine Zusammenarbeit bei Klassikern der „Schwarzen Serie" wie *Tote schlafen fest*, *Das unbekannte Gesicht* und *Gangster in Key Largo*.

1945 Er lässt sich von Mayo scheiden und heiratet Bacall.

1946 Ein neuer Vertrag mit Warner Bros. räumt ihm ein Vetorecht bei allen Projekten des Ehepaars ein und macht ihn zu einem der höchstbezahlten Stars in Hollywood.

1947 Bogart, Bacall und andere Schauspieler gehen nach Washington, um gegen die „Hexenjagd" des HUAC zu protestieren.

1948 Bogart gründet seine eigene Produktionsgesellschaft unter dem Namen Santana. Er spielt die Hauptrolle in John Hustons Klassiker *Der Schatz der Sierra Madre*.

1949 Bogarts Sohn Stephen wird geboren.

1950 Bogart produziert einen der wichtigsten Beiträge zum Genre des *Film noir* und spielt auch die Hauptrolle: *Ein einsamer Ort* unter der Regie von Nicholas Ray.

1952 Er erhält einen „Academy Award" („Oscar") für *African Queen*. Seine Tochter Leslie Howard (benannt nach dem Kollegen) wird geboren.

1954 Er spielt den psychisch gestörten Queeg in *Die Caine war ihr Schicksal* und wird dafür von der Kritik gefeiert.

1956 Er erkrankt an Speiseröhrenkrebs.

1957 Humphrey DeForest Bogart stirbt am 14. Januar.

CHRONOLOGIE

1899 Humphrey DeForest Bogart naît le 25 décembre à New York d'une mère peintre, Maud Humphrey, et d'un père médecin, Belmont Bogart.

1918 Humphrey est renvoyé de la prestigieuse Phillips Academy en raison de ses résultats médiocres.

1920 Employé comme garçon de bureau chez World Films, il se voit confier la réalisation de *Life* mais est finalement congédié.

1922 Fait ses débuts à Broadway dans la pièce *Drifting*.

1926 Épouse la star de Broadway Helen Menken.

1928 Épouse l'actrice Mary Philips.

1930 Mécontent de sa carrière théâtrale, Bogart signe avec la Fox et déménage à Los Angeles, où il n'obtient toutefois qu'une série de rôles sans intérêt.

1932 Il signe avec Columbia. N'obtenant là encore que des rôles mineurs, il se partage entre la scène et l'écran.

1935 Interprète Duke Mantee dans la pièce de Robert E. Sherwood *La Forêt pétrifiée*. Leslie Howard insiste pour qu'il joue également dans l'adaptation cinématographique de la pièce. Bogart signe un contrat avec la Warners.

1937 Incarne le gangster Baby Face Martin dans *Rue sans issue* de William Wyler. Divorce de Mary.

1938 Pendant le tournage du *Mystérieux Docteur Clitterhouse*, il rencontre John Huston, le scénariste, dont il restera toute sa vie l'ami et le compagnon de beuverie. En août, il épouse Mayo Methot.

1940 Bogart déclare devant la Commission parlementaire sur les activités anti-américaines qu'il n'a jamais été membre du Parti communiste.

1941 Grâce au succès critique et commercial de *La Grande Évasion*, Bogart se voit proposer des rôles plus importants et plus complexes. Il obtient le premier rôle dans l'adaptation par John Huston

du *Faucon maltais* de Dashiell Hammett, qui est également un succès.

1942 *Casablanca* fait un tabac au box-office, confirmant le statut d'icône de Humphrey Bogart dans le rôle de Rick Blaine, antihéros de film noir.

1944 Sur le tournage du *Port de l'angoisse*, Bogart rencontre un mannequin d'à peine vingt ans, Lauren Bacall. Il entame une liaison avec celle qui sera sa partenaire dans des classiques du film noir tels que *Le Grand Sommeil*, *Les Passagers de la nuit* et *Key Largo*.

1945 Divorce de Mayo et épouse Lauren Bacall.

1946 Un nouveau contrat avec la Warner lui confère un droit de veto sur ses films et fait de lui l'une des stars les mieux payées de Hollywood.

1947 Bogart, Bacall et d'autres acteurs se rendent à Washington pour protester contre la « chasse aux sorcières » menée au sein de l'industrie cinématographique.

1948 Bogart monte sa propre maison de production, Santana. Il joue dans un classique de John Huston, *Le Trésor de la Sierra Madre*.

1949 Naissance de son fils Stephen.

1950 Bogart produit et interprète l'un des chefs-d'œuvre du film noir, *Le Violent*, réalisé par Nicholas Ray.

1952 Remporte un oscar pour *L'Odyssée de l'African Queen*. Naissance de sa fille Leslie Howard (ainsi baptisée en l'honneur de l'acteur).

1954 Son interprétation du personnage psychologiquement instable de Queeg dans *Ouragan sur le Caine* lui vaut des critiques dithyrambiques.

1956 Contracte un cancer de l'œsophage.

1957 Humphrey DeForest Bogart décède le 14 janvier.

PORTRAIT (1947)

4

FILMOGRAPHY

FILMOGRAFIE

FILMOGRAPHIE

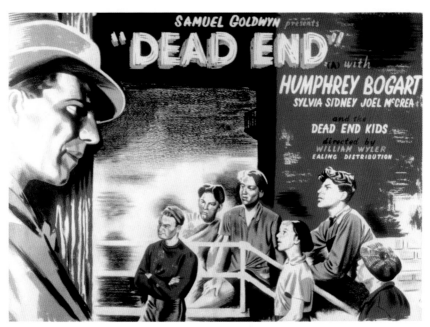

Life (1920)
Bit Part/Komparsenrolle/figuration.
Director/Regie/réalisation: Travers Vale.

The Dancing Town (1928)

Broadway's Like That (1930)
Director/Regie/réalisation: Murray Roth.

A Devil with Women (1930)
Tom Standish. Director/Regie/réalisation: Irving
Cummings.

Up the River (1930)
Steve. Director/Regie/réalisation: John Ford.

Body and Soul (1931)
Jim Watson. Director/Regie/réalisation: Alfred Santell.

Bad Sister (1931)
Valentine Corliss. Director/Regie/réalisation: Hobart
Henley.

Women of All Nations (1931)
Stone (part cut/herausgeschnitten/coupé au
montage). Director/Regie/réalisation: Raoul Walsh.

A Holy Terror (dt. *Tod und Teufel*, 1931)
Steve Nash. Director/Regie/réalisation: Irving
Cummings.

Love Affair (1932)
Jim Leonard. Director/Regie/réalisation: Thornton
Freeland.

Big City Blues (1932)
Shep Adkins. Director/Regie/réalisation: Mervyn
LeRoy.

Three on a Match (fr. *Une allumette pour trois*, 1932)
Harve. Director/Regie/réalisation: Mervyn LeRoy.

Midnight (1934)
Gar Boni. Director/Regie/réalisation: Chester Erskine.

**The Petrified Forest (dt. *Der versteinerte Wald*,
fr. *La Forêt pétrifiée*, 1936)**
Duke Mantee. Director/Regie/réalisation: Archie
Mayo.

**Bullets or Ballots (dt. *Wem gehört die Stadt?*,
fr. *Guerre au crime*, 1936)**
Nick Fenner. Director/Regie/réalisation: William
Keighley.

**Two Against the World (dt. *Zwei gegen die Welt*,
1936)**
Sherry Scott. Director/Regie/réalisation: William C.
McGann.

China Clipper (fr. *Courrier de Chine*, 1936)
Hap Stuart. Director/Regie/réalisation: Ray Enright.

Isle of Fury (fr. *L'Île de la furie*, 1936)
Val Stevens. Director/Regie/réalisation: Frank McDonald.

Black Legion (dt. *Geheimbund „Schwarze Legion"*, fr. *La Légion noire*, 1937)
Frank Taylor. Director/Regie/réalisation: Archie Mayo.

The Great O'Malley (dt. *Ordnung ist das halbe Leben*, fr. *Septième district*, 1937)
John Phillips. Director/Regie/réalisation: William Dieterle.

Marked Woman (dt. *Die gezeichnete Frau* [aka *Mord im Nachtclub*], fr. *Femmes marquées*, 1937)
David Graham. Director/Regie/réalisation: Lloyd Bacon.

Kid Galahad (fr. *Le Dernier Round*, 1937)
Turkey Morgan. Director/Regie/réalisation: Michael Curtiz.

San Quentin (dt. *Flucht aus San Quentin*, fr. *Le Révolté*, 1937)
Joe Kennedy. Director/Regie/réalisation: Lloyd Bacon.

Dead End (dt. *Sackgasse* [aka *Im Schatten der Wolkenkratzer*], fr. *Rue sans issue*, 1937)
Baby Face Martin. Director/Regie/réalisation: William Wyler.

Stand-In (dt. *Mr. Dodd geht nach Hollywood*, fr. *Monsieur Dood part pour Hollywood*, 1937)
Doug Quintain. Director/Regie/réalisation: Tay Garnett.

Swing Your Lady (1938)
Ed Hatch. Director/Regie/réalisation: Ray Enright.

Crime School (dt. *Schule des Verbrechens*, fr. *L'École du crime*, 1938)
Mark Braden. Director/Regie/réalisation: Lewis Seiler.

Men Are Such Fools (fr. *Les Hommes sont si bêtes*, 1938)
Harry Galleon. Director/Regie/réalisation: Busby Berkeley.

The Amazing Dr. Clitterhouse (dt. *Das Doppelleben des Dr. Clitterhouse*, fr. *Le Mystérieux Docteur Clitterhouse*, 1938)
Rocks Valentine. Director/Regie/réalisation: Michael Curtiz.

Racket Busters (fr. *Menaces sur la ville*, 1938)
Czar Martin. Director/Regie/réalisation: Lloyd Bacon.

Angels with Dirty Faces (dt. *Chikago – Engel mit schmutzigen Gesichtern*, fr. *Les Anges aux figures sales*, 1938)
Jim Frazier. Director/Regie/réalisation: William Keighley.

King of the Underworld (fr. *Hommes sans loi*, 1939)
Joe Gurney. Director/Regie/réalisation: Lewis Seiler.

The Oklahoma Kid (fr. *Terreur à l'ouest*, 1939)
Whip McCord. Director/Regie/réalisation: Lloyd Bacon.

Dark Victory (dt. *Opfer einer großen Liebe*, fr. *Victoire sur la nuit*, 1939)
Michael O'Leary. Director/Regie/réalisation: Edmund Goulding.

You Can't Get Away with Murder (fr. *Le Châtiment*, 1939)
Frank Wilson. Director/Regie/réalisation: Lewis Seiler.

The Roaring Twenties (dt. *Die wilden Zwanziger*, fr. *Les Fantastiques Années 20*, 1939)
George Hally. Director/Regie/réalisation: Raoul Walsh.

The Return of Dr. X (dt. *Das zweite Leben des Dr. X*, fr. *Le Retour du docteur X*, 1939)
Dr. Xavier. Director/Regie/réalisation: Vincent Sherman.

Invisible Stripes (dt. *Zwölf Monate Bewährungsfrist*, 1939)
Chuck Martin. Director/Regie/réalisation: Lloyd Bacon.

Virginia City (dt. *Goldschmuggel nach Virginia*, fr. *La Caravane héroïque*, 1940)
John Murrell. Director/Regie/réalisation: Michael Curtiz.

It All Came True (dt. *Ein Nachtclub für Sarah Jane*, fr. *Rendez-vous à minuit*, 1940)
Grasselli. Director/Regie/réalisation: Lewis Seiler.

Brother Orchid (dt. *Orchid, der Gangsterbruder*, 1940)
Jack Buck. Director/Regie/réalisation: Lloyd Bacon.

They Drive by Night (dt. *Sie fuhren bei Nacht* [aka *Nachts unterwegs*], fr. *Une femme dangereuse*, 1940)
Paul Fabrini. Director/Regie/réalisation: Raoul Walsh.

High Sierra (dt. *Entscheidung in der Sierra*, fr. *La Grande Évasion*, 1941)
Roy Earle. Director/Regie/réalisation: Raoul Walsh.

The Wagons Roll at Night (dt. *Von Stadt zu Stadt* [aka *Die Löwen reißen aus*], fr. *L'Amour et la Bête*, 1941)
Nick Coster. Director/Regie/réalisation: Ray Enright.

The Maltese Falcon (dt. *Die Spur des Falken* [aka *Der Malteser Falke*], fr. *Le Faucon maltais*, 1941)
Sam Spade. Director/Regie/réalisation: John Huston.

All Through the Night (dt. *Agenten der Nacht*, fr. *Échec à la Gestapo*, 1942)
Gloves Donahue. Director/Regie/réalisation: Vincent Sherman.

In This Our Life (dt. *Ich will mein Leben leben*, fr. *L'Amour n'est pas un jeu*, 1942)
Bit Part/Komparsenrolle/figuration. Director/Regie/réalisation: John Huston.

The Big Shot (dt. *Der große Gangster*, fr. *Le Caïd*, 1942)
Duke Berne. Director/Regie/réalisation: Lewis Seiler.

Across the Pacific (dt. *Abenteuer in Panama*, fr. *Griffes jaunes*, 1942)
Rick Leland. Director/Regie/réalisation: John Huston.

Casablanca (1942)
Rick Blaine. Director/Regie/réalisation: Michael Curtiz.

Action in the North Atlantic (dt. *Einsatz im Nordatlantik* [aka *Unterwegs nach Murmansk*], fr. *Convoi vers la Russie*, 1943)
Joe Rossi. Director/Regie/réalisation: Lloyd Bacon.

Sahara (fr. *Les Diables du Sahara*, 1943)
Joe Gunn. Director/Regie/réalisation: Zoltan Korda.

Passage to Marseille (dt. *Fahrkarte nach Marseille*, fr. *Passage pour Marseille*, 1944)
Jean Matrac. Director/Regie/réalisation: Michael Curtiz.

To Have and Have Not (dt. *Haben und Nichthaben*, fr. *Le Port de l'angoisse*, 1944)
Steve Morgan. Director/Regie/réalisation: Howard Hawks.

Conflict (dt. *Konflikt* [aka *Tatort Springfield*], fr. *La Mort n'était pas au rendez-vous*, 1945)
Richard Mason. Director/Regie/réalisation: Curtis Bernhardt.

The Big Sleep (dt. *Tote schlafen fest* [aka *Der tiefe Schlaf*], fr. *Le Grand Sommeil*, 1946)
Philip Marlowe. Director/Regie/réalisation: Howard Hawks.

Dead Reckoning (dt. *Späte Sühne* [aka *Späte Reue/Ein Mensch verschwindet*], fr. *En marge de l'enquête*, 1947)
Warren Murdock. Director/Regie/réalisation: John Cromwell.

The Two Mrs. Carrolls (dt. *Die zweite Mrs. Carroll*, fr. *La Seconde Mme Carroll*, 1947)
Geoffrey Carroll. Director/Regie/réalisation: Peter Godfrey.

Dark Passage (dt. *Das unbekannte Gesicht* [aka *Die schwarze Natter/Ums eigene Leben*], fr. *Les Passagers de la nuit*, 1947)
Vincent Parry. Director/Regie/réalisation: Delmer Daves.

The Treasure of the Sierra Madre (dt. *Der Schatz der Sierra Madre*, fr. *Le Trésor de la Sierra Madre*, 1948)
Fred C. Dobbs. Director/Regie/réalisation: John Huston.

Key Largo (dt. *Gangster in Key Largo* [aka *Hafen des Lasters*], 1948)
Frank McCloud. Director/Regie/réalisation: John Huston.

Knock on Any Door (dt. *Vor verschlossenen Türen*, fr. *Les Ruelles du malheur*, 1949)
Andrew Morton. Director/Regie/réalisation: Nicholas Ray.

Tokyo Joe (dt. *Tokio-Joe*, 1949)
Joe Barrett. Director/Regie/réalisation: Stuart Heisler.

Chain Lightning (dt. *Des Teufels Pilot,* fr. *Pilote du diable,* 1950)
Matt Brennan. Director/Regie/réalisation: Stuart Heisler.

In a Lonely Place (dt. *Ein einsamer Ort,* fr. *Le Violent,* 1950)
Dixon Steele. Director/Regie/réalisation: Nicholas Ray.

The Enforcer (dt. *Der Tiger,* fr. *La Femme à abattre,* 1951)
Martin Ferguson. Director/Regie/réalisation: Bretaigne Windust.

Sirocco (dt. *Sirocco - Zwischen Kairo und Damaskus,* 1951)
Harry Smith. Director/Regie/réalisation: Curtis Bernhardt.

The African Queen (dt. *African Queen,* fr. *L'Odyssée de l'African Queen,* 1951)
Charlie Allnut. Director/Regie/réalisation: John Huston.

Deadline U.S.A. (dt. *Die Maske runter,* fr. *Bas les masques,* 1952)
Ed Hutcheson. Director/Regie/réalisation: Richard Brooks.

Battle Circus (dt. *Arzt im Zwielicht* [aka *Arzt im Fegefeuer*], fr. *Le Cirque infernal,* 1953)
Jed Webbe. Director/Regie/réalisation: Richard Brooks.

The Jack Benny Program (TV 1953)
Babyface Bogart.

Beat the Devil (dt. *Schach dem Teufel,* fr. *Plus fort que le diable,* 1953)
Billy Dannreuther. Director/Regie/réalisation: John Huston.

The Caine Mutiny (dt. *Die Caine war ihr Schicksal,* fr. *Ouragan sur le Caine,* 1954)
Philip Queeg. Director/Regie/réalisation: Edward Dmytryk.

Sabrina (1954)
Linus Larrabee. Director/Regie/réalisation: Billy Wilder.

Love Lottery (dt. *Liebeslotterie,* fr. *La Loterie de l'amour,* 1954)
Uncredited/Cameo-Auftritt/non crédité.
Director/Regie/réalisation: Charles Crichton.

The Barefoot Contessa (dt. *Die barfüßige Gräfin,* fr. *La Comtesse aux pieds nus,* 1954)
Harry Dawes. Director/Regie/réalisation: Joseph L. Mankiewicz.

The Petrified Forest (TV 1955)
Duke Mantee. Director/Regie/réalisation: Delbert Mann.

We're No Angels (dt. *Wir sind keine Engel,* fr. *La Cuisine des anges,* 1955)
Joseph. Director/Regie/réalisation: Michael Curtiz.

The Left Hand of God (dt. *Die linke Hand Gottes,* fr. *La Main gauche du Seigneur,* 1955)
Jim Carmody. Director/Regie/réalisation: Edward Dmytryk.

The Desperate Hours (dt. *An einem Tag wie jeder andere,* fr. *La Maison des otages,* 1955)
Glenn Griffin. Director/Regie/réalisation: William Wyler.

The Harder They Fall (dt. *Schmutziger Lorbeer,* fr. *Plus dure sera la chute,* 1956)
Eddie Willis. Director/Regie/réalisation: Mark Robson.

BIBLIOGRAPHY

Agusti, P.: *Humphrey Bogart.* Edimat Libros, 1998.

Bacall, Lauren: *By Myself.* Knopf, 1980.

Bacall, Lauren: *Now.* Knopf, 1994.

Barbour, Alan: *Humphrey Bogart.* Pyramid, 1973.

Benchley, Nathaniel: *Humphrey Bogart.* Little, Brown, 1975.

Bogart, Stephen Humphrey: *Bogart: In Search of My Father.* Dutton, 1995.

Brooks, Louise: *Lulu in Hollywood.* Knopf, 1982.

Cahill, Marie: *Humphrey Bogart.* Smithmark Publishers, 1993.

Coe, Jonathan: *Humphrey Bogart: Take It & Like It.* Grove Press, 1991.

Cunningham, Ernest W.: *The Ultimate Bogart.* Renaissance Books, 1999.

Duchovnay, Gerald: *Humphrey Bogart.* Greenwood Press, 1999.

Eyles, Allen: *Bogart.* Doubleday, 1975.

Frank, Alan: *Humphrey Bogart.* Bookthrift, 1982.

Goodman, Ezra: Bogey: *The Good-Bad Guy.* Lyle Stuart, 1965.

Hepburn, Katharine: *The Making of African Queen: Or How I Went to Africa with Bogart, Bacall, and Huston and Almost Lost My Mind.* Knopf, 1987.

Huston, John: *Humphrey Bogart.* Seiler Press, 1957.

Hyams, Joe: *Bogart and Bacall: A Love Story.* McKay, 1975.

Hyams, Joe: *Bogie.* New American Library, 1966.

McCarty, Clifford: *The Complete Films of Humphrey Bogart.* Citadel Press, 1994.

Meyers, Jeffrey: *Bogart: A Life in Hollywood.* Houghton Mifflin, 1997.

Michael, Paul: *Humphrey Bogart: The Man and His Films.* Bonanza Books, 1965.

Pettigrew, Terence: *Bogart: A Definitive Study of His Film Career.* Proteus, 1977.

Porter, Darwin: *The Secret Life of Humphrey Bogart: The Early Years.* Georgia Literary Assocation, 2003.

Ruddy, Jonah & Hill, Jonathan: *The Bogey Man: Portrait of a Legend.* Souvenir Press, 1965.

Schickel, Richard: *Bogie: A Celebration of the Life and Films of Humphrey Bogart.* Dunne, 2006.

Sklar, Robert: *City Boys: Cagney, Bogart, Garfield.* Princeton University, 1992.

Sperber, A.M. & Lax, Eric: *Bogart.* William Morrow, 1997.

Tchernoff, Alexis: *Humphrey Bogart.* Pygmalion, 1985.

Thain, Andrea: *Humphrey Bogart.* Wunderlich, 1996.

Thompson, Verita with Donald Shepherd: *Bogie and Me: A Love Story.* St. Martin's Press, 1982.

Viertel, Peter: Dangerous Friends: *At Large with Huston and Hemingway in the Fifties.* Doubleday, 1992.

IMPRINT

© 2007 TASCHEN GmbH
Hohenzollernring 53, D-50672 Köln
www.taschen.com

Editor/Picture Research/Layout: Paul Duncan/Wordsmith Solutions
Editorial Coordination: Martin Holz, Cologne
Production Coordination: Nadia Najm and Horst Neuzner, Cologne
German Translation: Thomas J. Kinne, Nauheim
French Translation: Anne Le Bot, Paris
Multilingual Production: www.arnaudbriand.com, Paris
Typeface Design: Sense/Net, Andy Disl and Birgit Reber, Cologne

Printed in Italy
ISBN 978-3-8228-2118-3

To stay informed about upcoming TASCHEN titles, please
request our magazine at www.taschen.com/magazine or write to
TASCHEN, Hohenzollernring 53, D-50672 Cologne, Germany,
contact@taschen.com, Fax: +49-221-254919. We will be happy to
send you a free copy of our magazine which is filled with infor-
mation about all of our books.